Working Drawings *of* Colonial Furniture

by

Frederick J. Bryant

Supervisor of Manual Arts

Auburn, Maine

The Manual Arts Press

Peoria, Illinois

1922

A Facsimile Reprint From

The Toolemera Press

www.toolemera.com

Working Drawings of Colonial Furniture, by Frederick J. Bryant
Originally published by The Manual Arts Press, Peoria, Illinois, 1922.

No part of this book may be reproduced, stored in an electronic retrieval system, or transmitted in any form or by an means, electronic, mechanical, photocopy, photographic or otherwise without the written permission of the publisher. Excerpts of one page or less for the purposes of review and comment are permissible.

Copyright © 2010 The Toolemera Press
All rights reserved.

International Standard Book Number
ISBN : 978-0-9825329-5-9

Published by
The Toolemera Press
Dedham, Massachusetts
U.S.A. 02026

Manufactured in the United States of America

The Toolemera Press produces facsimile reprints of classic titles on early tools, trades, crafts and industries. All titles are drawn from our personal library.

A facsimile reprint reproduces the look and feel of the original book. When appropriate, original hand written notations, paper texture, owner/author markings, pagination and page orientation are maintained in the reprint. Covers are reproduced in full color to match the originals.

Many early books were printed in a smaller format than is typical of modern books. Paper was expensive, as was the entire process of publishing a book. Some Toolemera Press reprints are reproduced to size while others are enlarged, in proportion to the original, to increase the legibility of graphic or textual details.

WORKING DRAWINGS
of
COLONIAL FURNITURE
by

FREDERICK J. BRYANT
SUPERVISOR OF MANUAL ARTS
AUBURN, MAINE

THE MANUAL ARTS PRESS
PEORIA, ILLINOIS

Copyright 1922
Frederick J. Bryant
43P81

Printed in the United States of America

PREFACE

BECAUSE of the increasing demand for woodworking projects embracing the designs of the famous masters, Chippendale, Hepplewhite, and Sheraton, the author has endeavored to secure dimensioned sketches and photographs of old fashioned furniture. While this collection does not represent the highest types, there are features in all which merit distinction. Only those which could be copied by junior and senior high-school students have been considered. Nothing has been added to or detracted from the original measurements.

It is hoped that these drawings and illustrations will afford an inspiration for instructors and students. For reference work, *Woodwork for Secondary Schools*, by I. S. Griffith, (The Manual Arts Press, Peoria, Ill.) will prove of great value.

While this book is designed for use in the schools, it need not be so confined. Its scope and practical treatment should fit it for the use of all who enjoy the pleasure of creating things of wood.

Acknowledgment is made to the magazine *The House Beautiful* for the use of one of the illustrations.

FREDERICK J. BRYANT.

Auburn, Maine, July 1921

In Such a House Colonial Furniture is Found

CONTENTS

	PAGE
Gate-Leg Table	7
Sheraton Card Table	10
Sheraton Work Table	12
Sheraton Breakfast Table	14
Tavern Table	16
Mahogany Tea Table	18
Hepplewhite Work Table	20
Hepplewhite Card Table	22
Empire Card Table	24
Mahogany Tip-Top Table	26
Grandfather Clock	31
Banjo Clock	36
Windsor Chairs	38
Hepplewhite Chair	44
Empire Chair	46
Colonial Looking Glass	48
Old Fashioned Mirror	50
Wood Finishing	52

Gate-leg Table and Bannister-back Chair Belonging to the Oliver Family, Scarboro, Me. Date Back to 1680. Passed Down in Family for Eight Generations

GATE-LEG TABLE

DUE to the present popularity of period furniture designs, the demand for gate-leg tables has almost become a fad. Thousands of reproductions have been made and the style has been highly featured in magazines and books of recent publication. During the Colonial days the tables were often made of oak. William Penn owned one of this kind. Later models were made of walnut and maple. Most of them are now made of mahogany, walnut, gum and birch. Those made of other woods like poplar or whitewood and pine are often finished in tones of ivory, cream or gray, with decorative patterns stenciled on the top surface.

DIRECTIONS FOR MAKING THE TABLE

To reproduce the table shown on these drawings, turn the legs and stretchers on the lathe. Cut out the stock to dimensions for other parts of the table and then proceed with the assembly of the end frames. Cut the notches and glue up the two gates. Locate and bore the pivot centers and cut the notches on the cross-rails and long stretchers. It is advisable to put the rest of the table together, using clamps, but no glue. This is to see if all parts are properly placed and if the gates are hung correctly. Testing with a steel square will help to check up the work. If the table frame and gates all rest evenly on the floor, either in open or closed position, the joints are ready for glueing. A drawer 24" deep is made to slide in on one end, and a drawer pull similar to No. 2 on page 28 should be used. All the joints are mortised and tenoned and also doweled. The appearance of dowels on the outside is not objectionable on gate-leg or tavern tables. The top is oval in shape and has beaded edges to match the leaves. Plain butt hinges are fastened to the underside of the leaves and table top. The finish is one of choice and depends largely on the kind of wood used to make the table. The original one is made of maple and is stained a dark brown color.

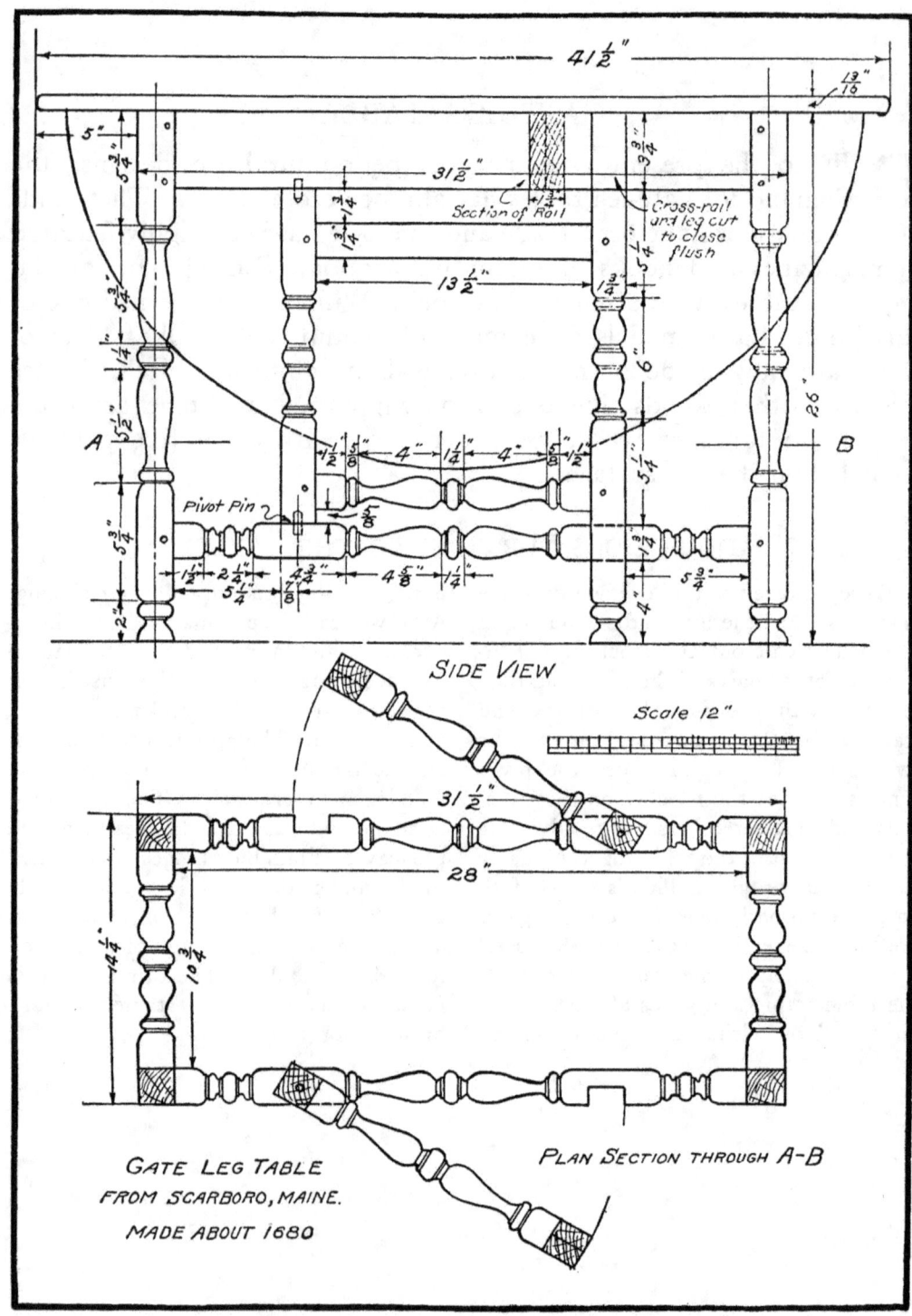

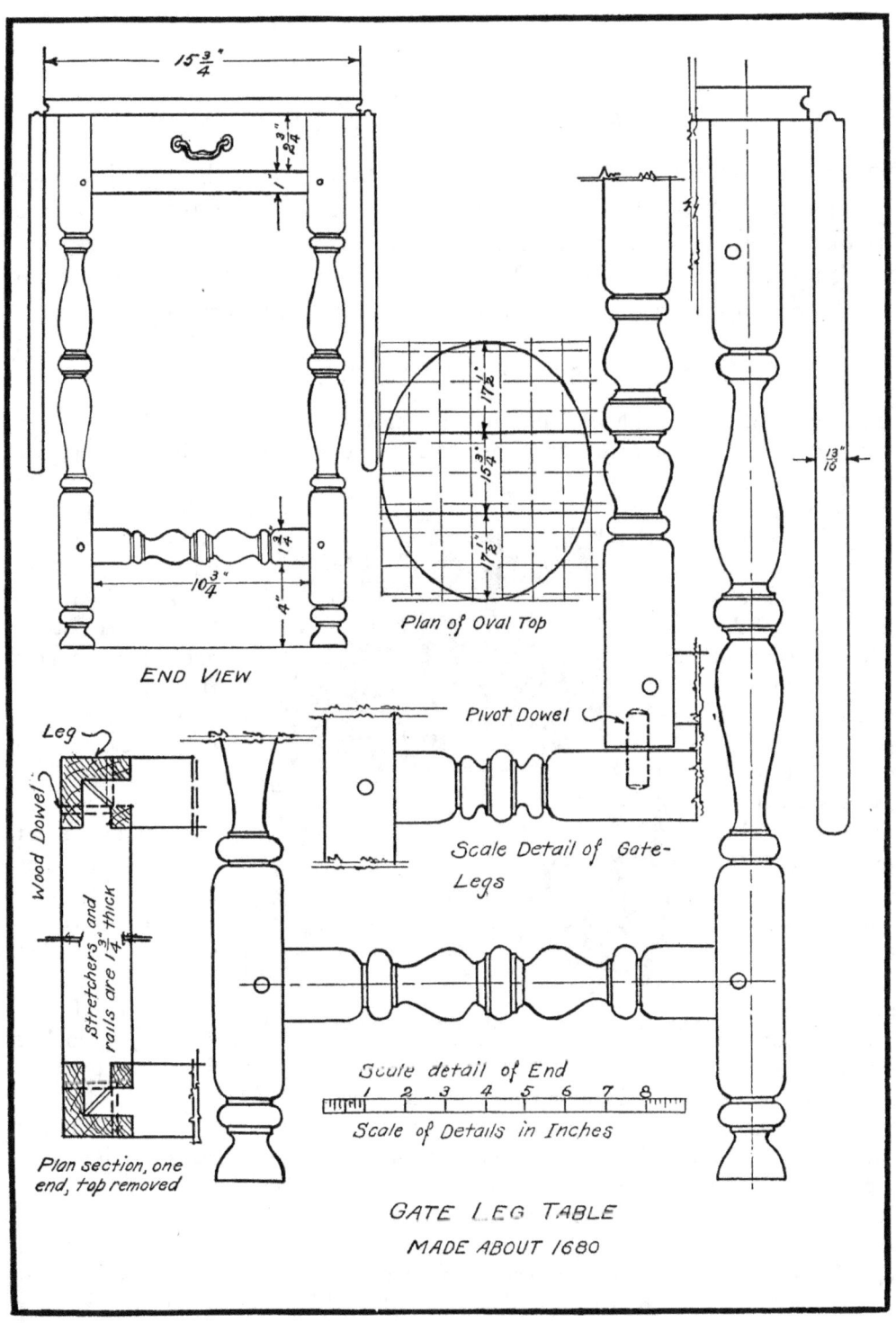

PLATE II

SHERATON CARD TABLE

IN many instances it is rather difficult to distinguish the difference between Hepplewhite and Sheraton designs. Sheraton published a book in 1791 and another in 1804. He no doubt was influenced by the designs of Hepplewhite. His early work was much better than that which appeared near the close of the eighteenth century.

DIRECTIONS FOR MAKING THE TABLE

In some respects this table is similar in construction to the one on page 23. The legs instead of being square are round and reeded, or fluted, as it is often called. To make a reproduction of this table, first cut four pieces of mahogany for the legs. Two of these pieces should have a quarter-section removed so that they can be easily fastened to the table frame on the front side. Temporary pieces can be glued into these places while the legs are being turned on the lathe. The reeding can be done by hand. Mark off a strip of paper into twelve equal parts, the paper being long enough to pass around the post where the reeding commences. Paste this strip on the wood at that point. Prepare another paper for the lower end of the legs where the reeding stops and after dividing this piece into the same number of parts, attach it to the posts in a like manner. All this can be done while the legs are in the lathe which will hold them securely. Be sure to have the ends of both paper strips in line with each other, and then connect the points on the upper strip with corresponding points on the lower one, using a straight-edge about 17" long. Draw the lines with a sharp point and pass over each line a number of times. Take two thin pieces of steel and shape them like Fig. 13 on page 29. Hold each one as firmly as possible and deepen the lines. A few strokes on each one will develop the reeds which can be sandpapered afterward.

The back legs are made up the same as the front legs except that they are square at the upper end where the rails are attached. The frame of the table is much like that of the Hepplewhite

A Sheraton Table which is Owned by William Gerrish, of Saco, Maine

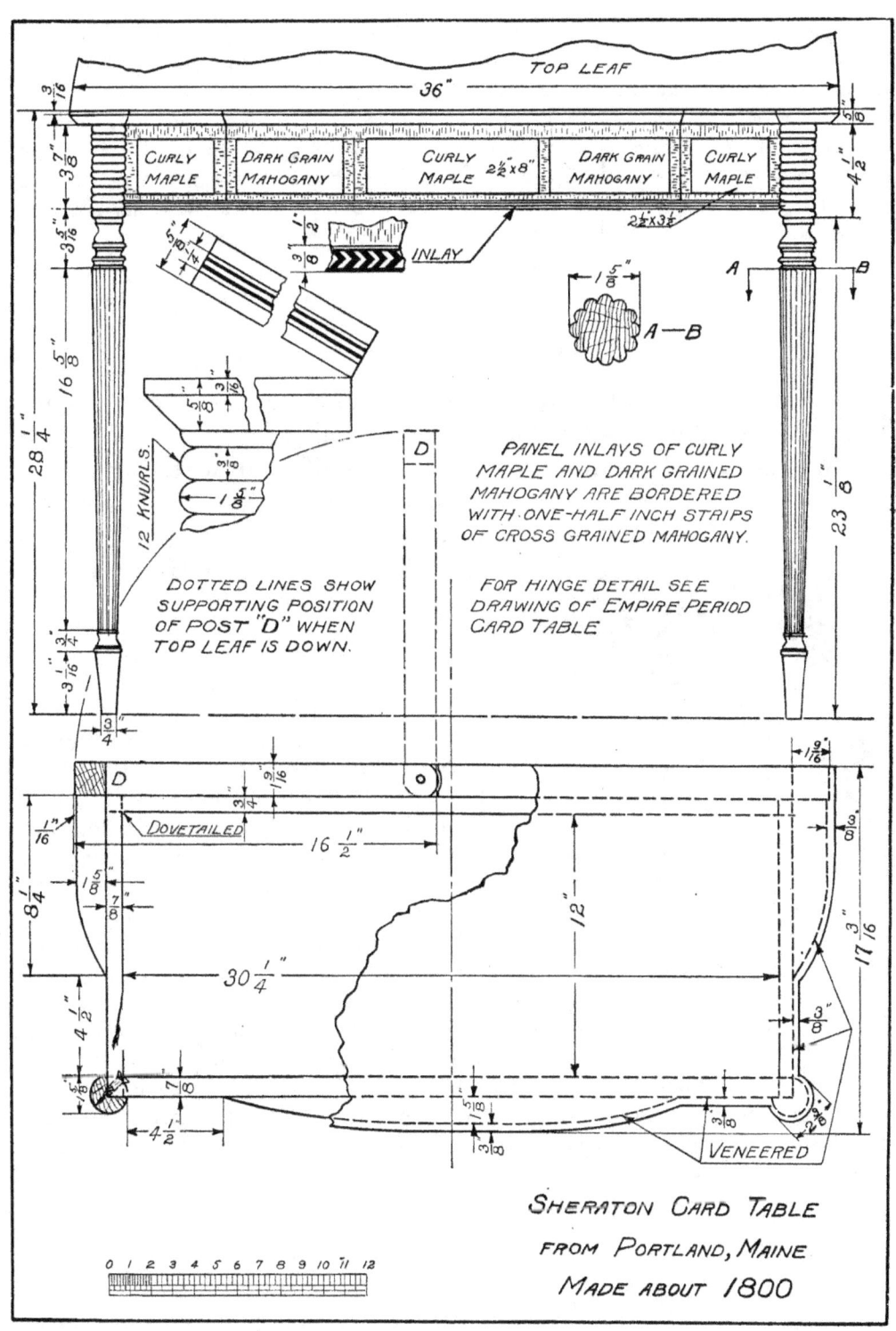

SHERATON CARD TABLE
FROM PORTLAND, MAINE
MADE ABOUT 1800

Plate III

table, page 23. The rails are pine with heavy pieces glued on the front and two ends. Mark out the curves which are shown on the drawing and band-saw close to the lines. Save the waste pieces and use them as cauls when glueing the veneers. The satinwood or maple marquetry panels should be glued in place and the borders afterward. These borders are ½" wide and are for the front only, so the end rails must be veneered with mahogany. The hinges are the same as shown in Fig. 10, page 29. The top is made up in two parts. The lower one is plain and the other is inlaid along the edge.

SHERATON WORK TABLE

THIS is the one table in this collection of drawings which should be the stepping-stone for the more difficult projects. It is quite small, has good lines and can be slightly modified from the drawing.

A Sheraton Work Table which is Easy to Reproduce, or which may be Modified

It is suggested that this table be made first by the student if he contemplates the making of any of the card tables.

DIRECTIONS FOR MAKING THE TABLE

Before turning the legs, cut out a quarter-section of the four legs down 6⅝" from the top and glue in temporary pieces. Locate the centers accurately on the lathe and turn down the wood to the proper dimensions. The table will look much better if the legs are reeded as described on page 10. When the legs are finished the table frame can be put together. To attach the legs, remove the temporary pieces and they can be screwed to the frame. A drawer with a veneered front should be made. The picture shows a wooden knob on the front. This should not be copied as it is not the original and belongs to a later style which developed near the close of the Empire period. A drawer pull similar to No. 11 on page 28 is suggested for the reproduction.

SHERATON WORK TABLE

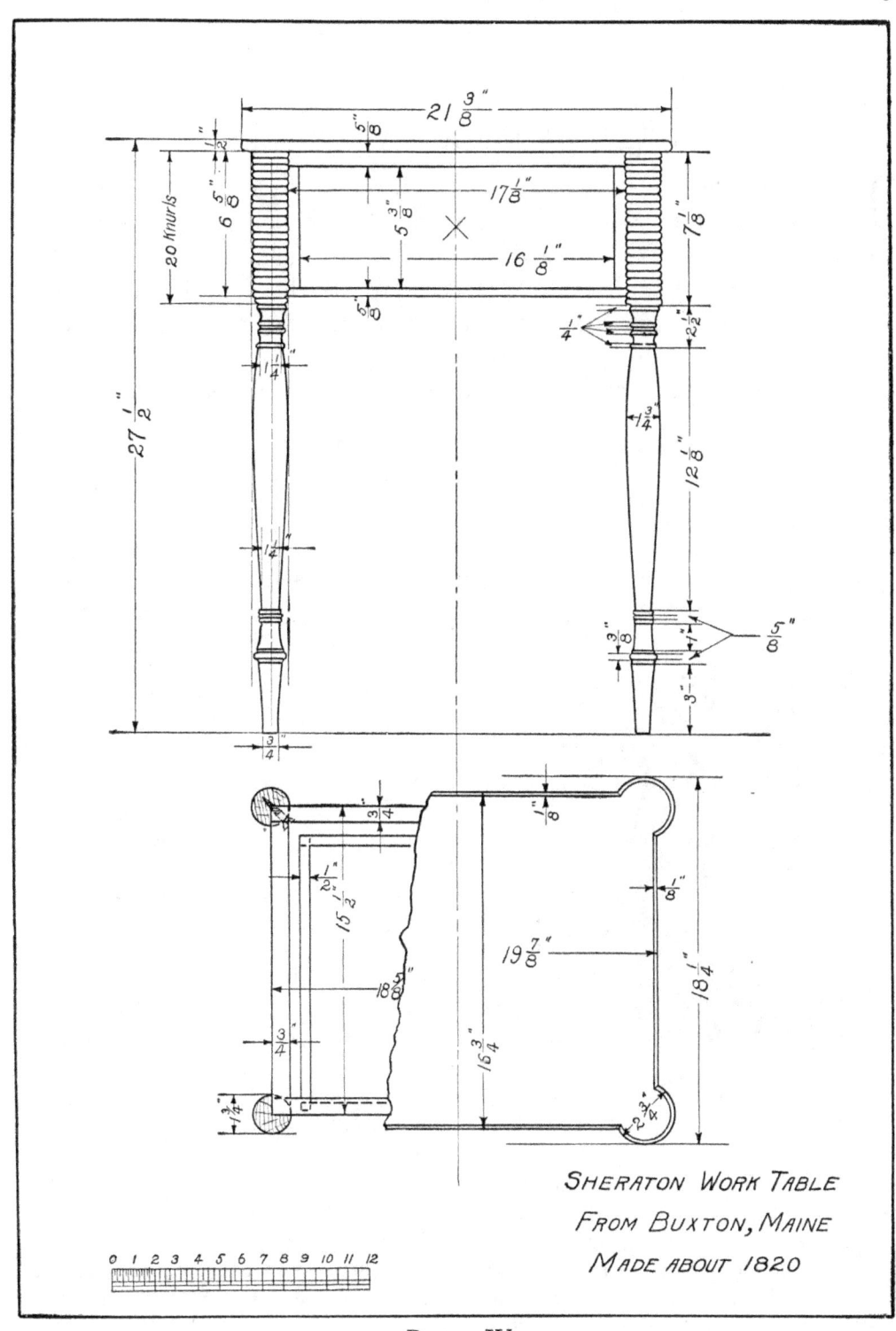

Sheraton Work Table
From Buxton, Maine
Made about 1820

Plate IV

SHERATON BREAKFAST TABLE

THIS table is one of very pleasing lines and is not a difficult project to make. While it is termed a breakfast table, there is no reason why it cannot find an appropriate place in any room. The characteristics of a table of this kind consist of the drop leaves, which are held up by wooden brackets that swing under the top. It is made of mahogany and has some inlay on the outer edges of the legs and border strips of inlay can be found along the lower edges of the rails.

DIRECTIONS FOR MAKING THE TABLE

Plane up the stock for the legs, making the tapers as shown. These should stop within $4\frac{1}{2}''$ of the top. It is advisable to cut the mortises before doing any inlay work as the lines may be injured in handling. The cross-rail in the rear is mahogany and the side-rails are made of pine with maple facing, part of which consists of the wooden hinges. Section $A—B$ on the drawing of the Hepplewhite card table, page 23, shows the details of such hinges.

Inlaying the legs with white holly lines is an easy process. An ordinary marking gage with the spur sharpened as shown in Fig. 12 on page 29 will cut and clean the grooves. The corners can be cleared by scoring lines with a sharp knife and removing the wood with the tang of a small file previously sharpened. Apply glue to three sides of the inlay and press it firmly into the grooves. The handle of a bench knife is useful for this. Remove enough wood for the insertion of the oval centers near the top of the legs and glue in place, using a clamp on each one. After they are dry, remove the clamps, carefully score and cut out the wood for the white holly border. These oval centers can be made by cutting out thin sheets of dark grained mahogany. If the veneer is dampened it will not crack.

If it is not possible to secure the ebony veneers for the bands around the lower ends of the legs, a fine imitation can be made by knifing the lines around the legs and then applying two or more thin coats of black shellac. The lines must be cut deep enough to prevent the color from running over the edges.

THIS SHERATON BREAKFAST TABLE CAN BE PUT TO A VARIETY OF USES. IT WAS NAMED "PEMBROKE" TABLE BY SHERATON, AFTER THE LADY FOR WHOM THE FIRST ONE WAS MADE

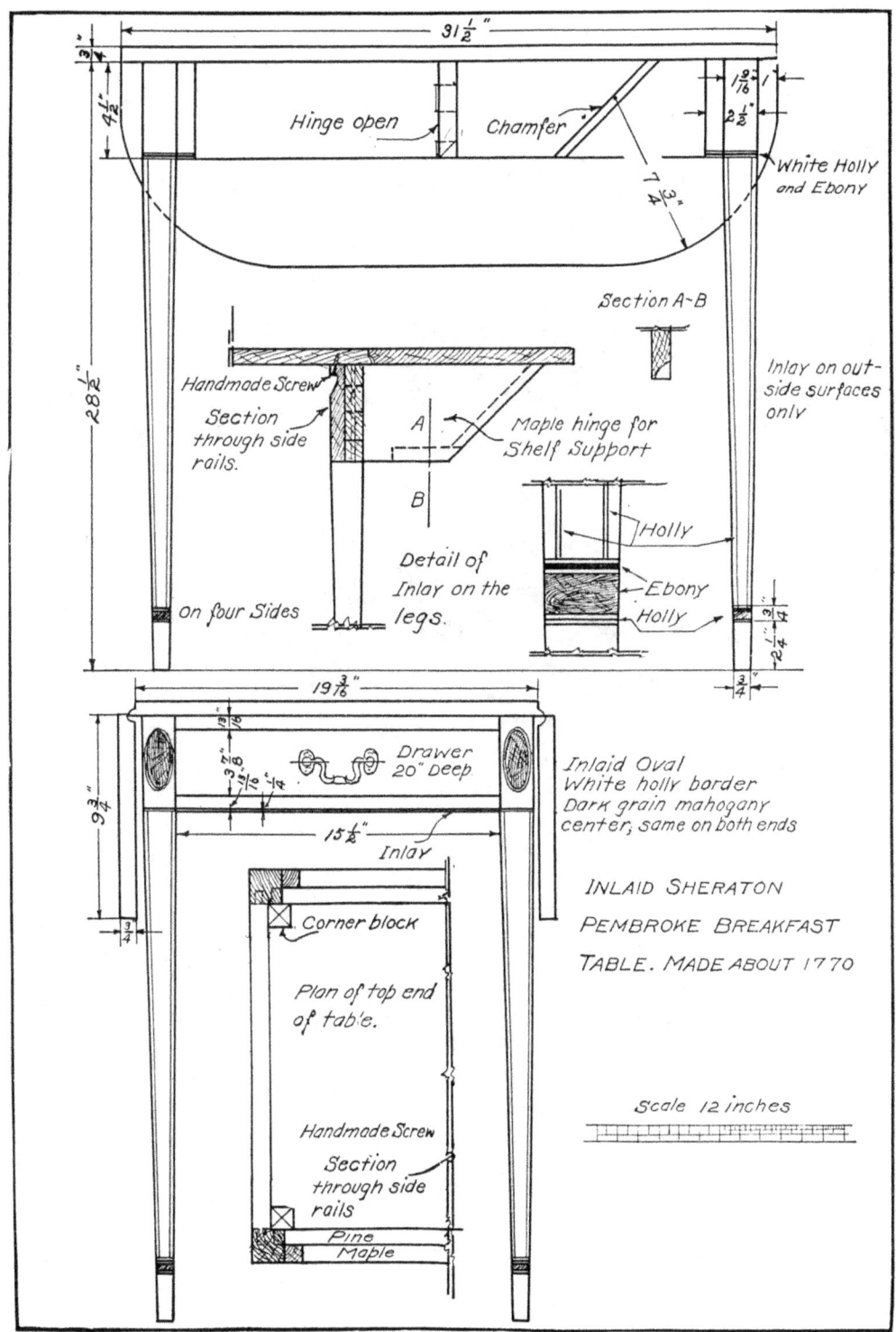

PLATE V

TAVERN TABLE

TAVERN tables are among the early types developed in this country and are eagerly sought for by collectors of the antique. Reproductions are quite common and are desirable in the modern home. The old tables were generally made with pine tops and maple legs and stretchers, and painted in almost any color. The present tendency is to follow the same design and improve the finish by using a higher grade cabinet wood, the staining and finishing being the same as for any other table. Dark shades may be used as well as light ones, especially if the wood used in the reproduction is of the same kind as specified in the drawing.

OLD TAVERN TABLE DISCOVERED AT BUXTON, MAINE, BY THE AUTHOR. IT WAS MADE ABOUT 1720

DIRECTIONS FOR MAKING THE TABLE

Glue up the stock for the top and while it is drying, the legs can be turned on the lathe. Make a full size lay-out of the end view of the table to determine the angles needed for the jointing of the cross rails under the top and the stretchers below. All the joints of the frame are mortised and tenoned and doweled. After the frame is put together, the top can be set in place as shown on the drawing, or the more modern way of fastening from the under side can be used. In the latter case the cleat is not essential but should be used to carry out the effect. It also may prevent the table top from warping out of shape due to the long overhang which extends beyond the sides of the table frame.

OLD TAVERN TABLE

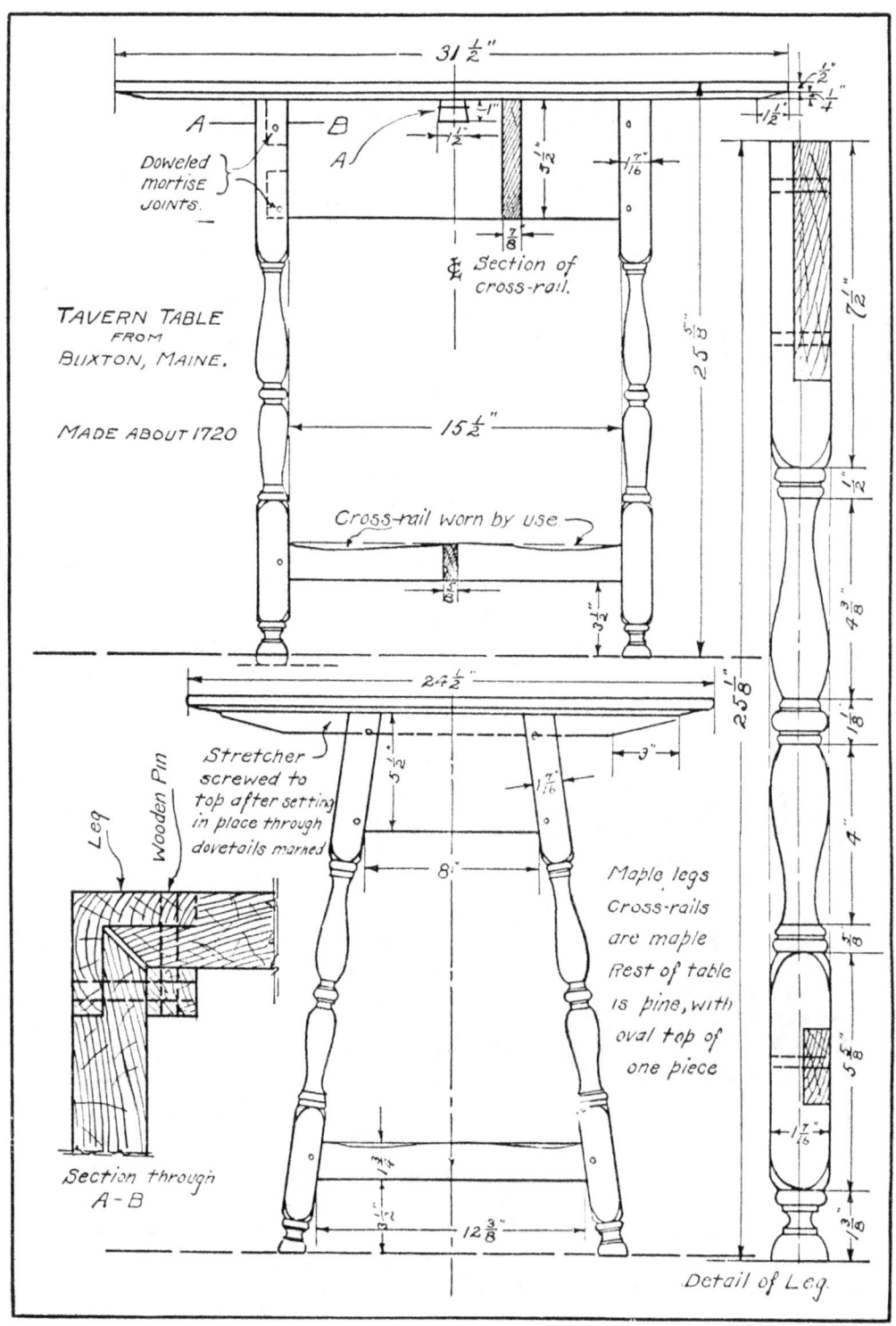

PLATE VI

MAHOGANY TEA TABLE

THIS drawing introduces another style which was very much in evidence during the Colonial days. Because of its singular form and beauty it is one of the best of the period designs. Mahogany is used throughout and the only inlay used is found along the edge of the top. The tripod base on this table is often called "snake foot" which distinguishes it somewhat from the shape of the base on the tip-top table.

DIRECTIONS FOR MAKING THE TABLE

It will take a piece of mahogany about 21" square to make the top. A heavy paper pattern of one side of the top can be used to make the outline the same on all sides. The top may be cut to shape on the band-saw. Smooth up the edges, and then with a sharp marking-gage score two lines around the edge. Remove the wood between the two lines and glue in the inlay border. If it shows any signs of cracking on the corners, dampen it. Rub the inlay firmly with the handle of a knife and wipe off any superfluous glue.

The pedestal should now be turned on the lathe. Any dimensions needed can be scaled from the drawing. Be sure to include a 1" pin on the upper end of the pedestal. This is for the square maple block which is placed on top. Measure up 2⅝" from the lower end and make a fine line with a pair of dividers. This line limits the highest position of the three feet. Parts of this line will show when the table is assembled, but it is present on all tables of this kind.

Take a sheet of cardboard and rule it off in 2" squares, and from the drawing reproduce the curves which form the outline of the feet. Allow ¾" for the dovetails. Cut out the pattern, trace it on wood, having the grain run the longest way and band-saw the pieces. Now taper the legs and round over the upper surfaces. A small thin piece of wood is glued to the base of each foot. To cut the dovetails on the pedestal and locate the feet proceed as follows: Take a narrow strip of paper equal in length to the cir-

TEA TABLE WITH "SNAKE FOOT" BASE

MAHOGANY TEA TABLE

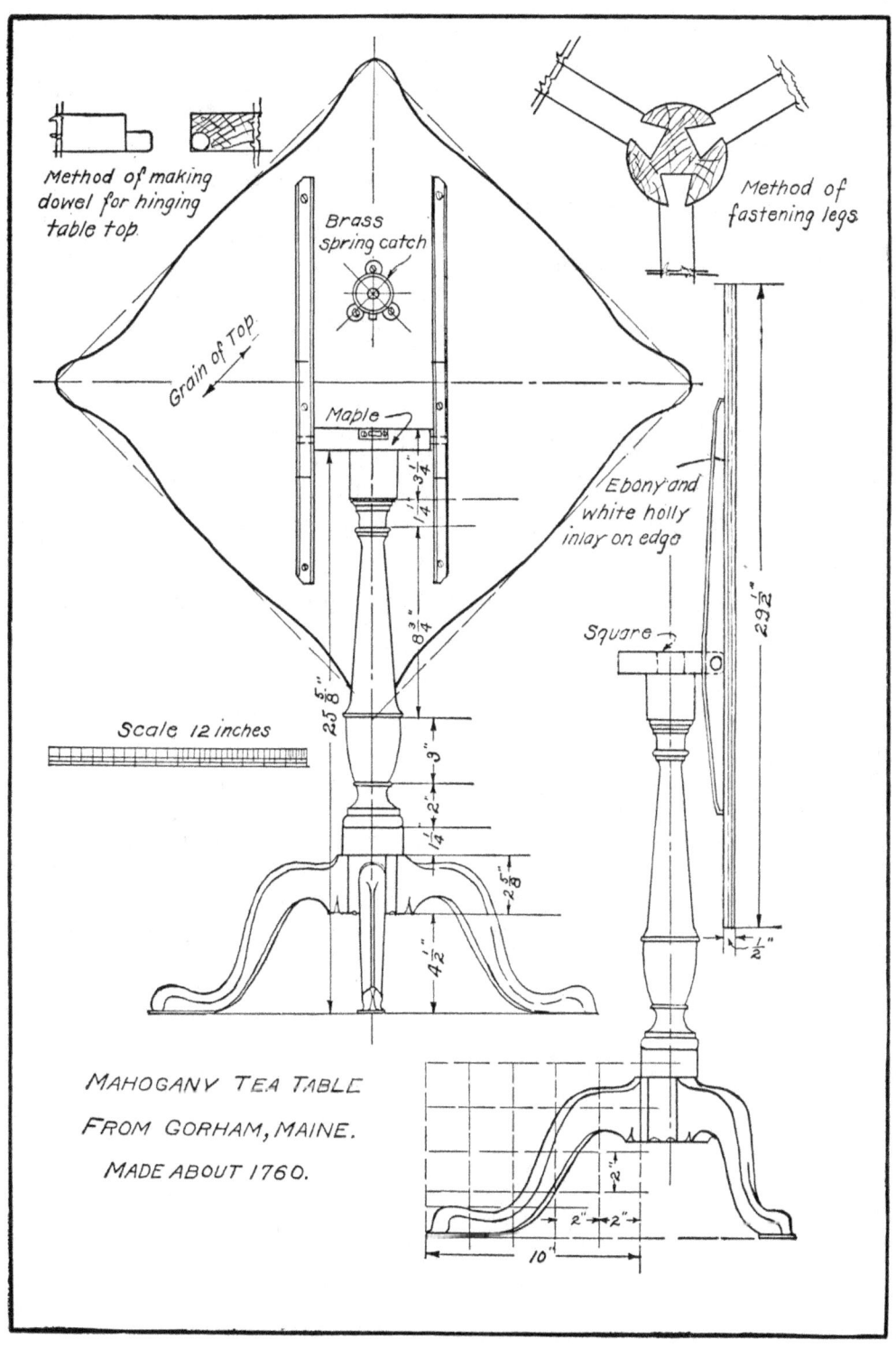

PLATE VII

cumference of the post and space it off into three equal parts with a pencil. Paste the strip around the post and transfer the marks on the wood. Now place the pedestal in a horizontal position in the vise and with a rule, draw lines thru these points. These are center lines. Measure from them on each side ⅝" and draw lines. The next step is to flatten these places where the feet are to be dovetailed. Lay out the dovetails on the ends of the post and the flattened area; and make up the joints. Glue the feet in place. Make the cleat for the underside of the top; also a maple block 5" square with a 1" hole thru the center and two pivot pins on the ends, as shown on the drawing. Locate the top so that it will swing down directly in front of one of the legs. The table will not tip over so easily if made this way. A metal catch locks the top down when in a horizontal position.

HEPPLEWHITE WORK TABLE

THIS table is made of mahogany and has the usual amount of inlay. The shape and design identify it with the Hepplewhite period. Like the card table, the legs are tapered, inlaid and banded near the bottom. There is one compartment on each end and a drawer in the center.

DIRECTIONS FOR MAKING THE TABLE

Follow the general directions for making the Hepplewhite card table on page 22. Make a drawer for the middle of the table and place what inlay is needed. Cut mortises on the ends of the posts to connect the half-circle compartments with the main frame. Five-ply stock is used for the ends and if this cannot be made or obtained, the curve can be bandsawed from thicker material. The bottom is set in on the underside and is ¼" thick. The ebony bands around the bottom of the posts are essential to this particular piece of furniture and directions and suggestions are given on page 14.

HEPPLEWHITE WORK TABLE

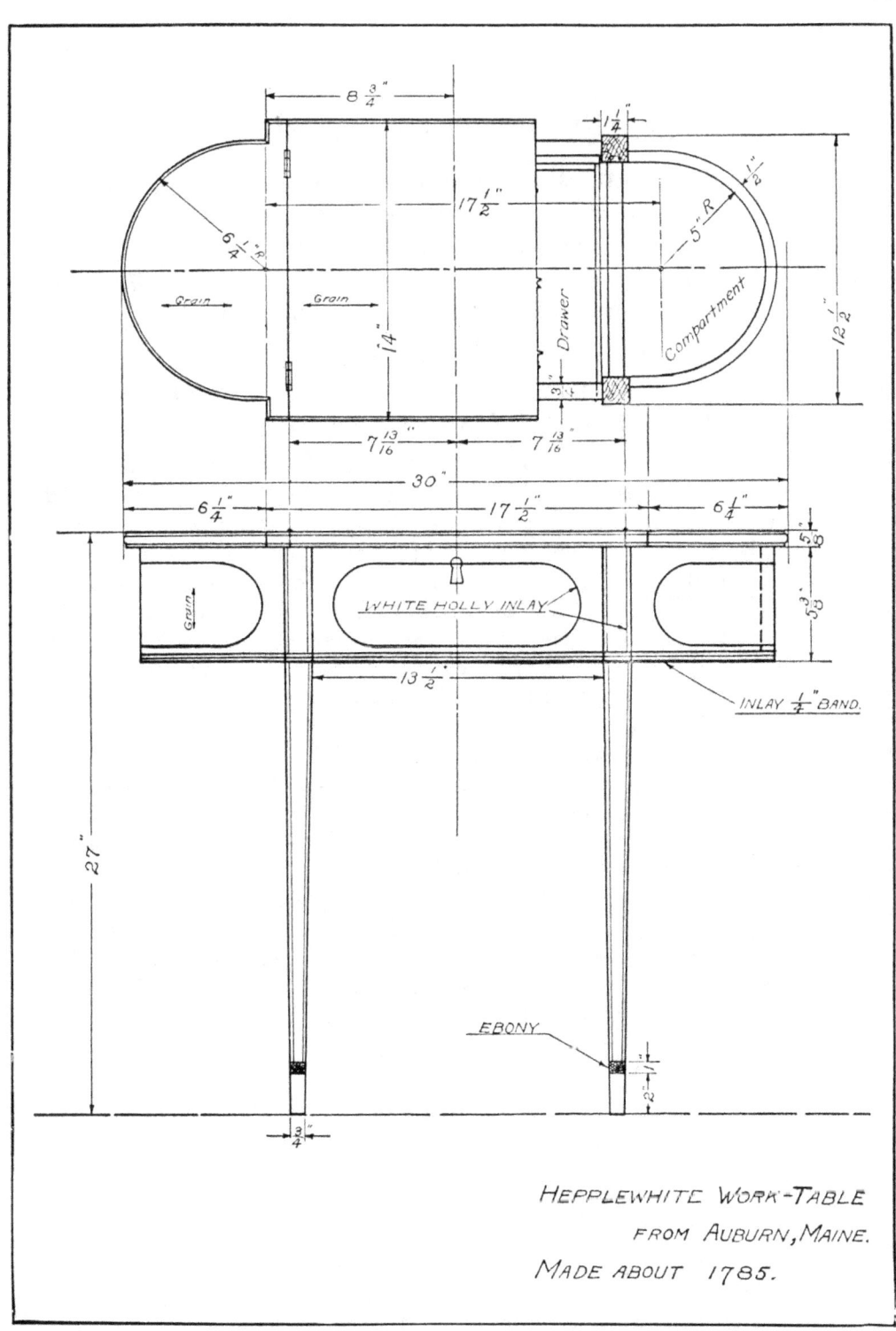

Plate VIII

HEPPLEWHITE CARD TABLE

MANY who are interested in antiques consider Hepplewhite's designs to be the best. He published a book in 1789 called, *The Cabinet-maker and Upholsterer's Guide, or Repository of Designs for Every Article of Household Furniture in the Newest and Most Approved Taste*. His chairs, sideboards, and tables represent his best efforts. They are graceful, beautifully inlaid and delicate in appearance.

DIRECTIONS FOR MAKING THE TABLE

Plane and taper the four posts and inlay the front and outer surfaces. Stop the inlay about 3" from the bottom and copy the ebony border which is shown on the drawing of the Breakfast Table on page 14. If the ebony veneer cannot be obtained, follow the suggestions offered on that page. The directions for inlaying are the same. Use well seasoned pine or other soft wood for the rails which are to be veneered. Dovetail the joints where the movable post is and glue corner blocks to further strengthen the frame. Two heavy pieces of pine are glued and screwed to the front posts and end rails. The back rail of pine is reinforced with a piece of maple (see Fig. 9 on page 29) half of which is mortised to the movable post and hinged about midway. The remaining half is fastened to the table frame. A detail of the wooden hinge can be found on the drawing, Section *A—B*. Use sheet veneer to cover the pine rails and after it is dry, part of it can be cut away for the border which passes along the lower edge. Use a marking gage with a spur as shown in Fig. 12 on page 29 to cut the grooves for the inlay lines.

The table top is made up in two parts. The first one is plain and has no inlay. It extends $\frac{3}{8}$" beyond all parts of the frame and posts and has a concave bevel on the under side. The other has a square edge and a narrow inlay border as shown in the detail. The hinges are made of brass and are placed on the ends. For dimensions see the drawing of the Empire Card Table on page 25, and Fig. 10 on page 29. For detail of inlay at the lower end of the legs, see plate V.

HEPPLEWHITE CARD TABLE

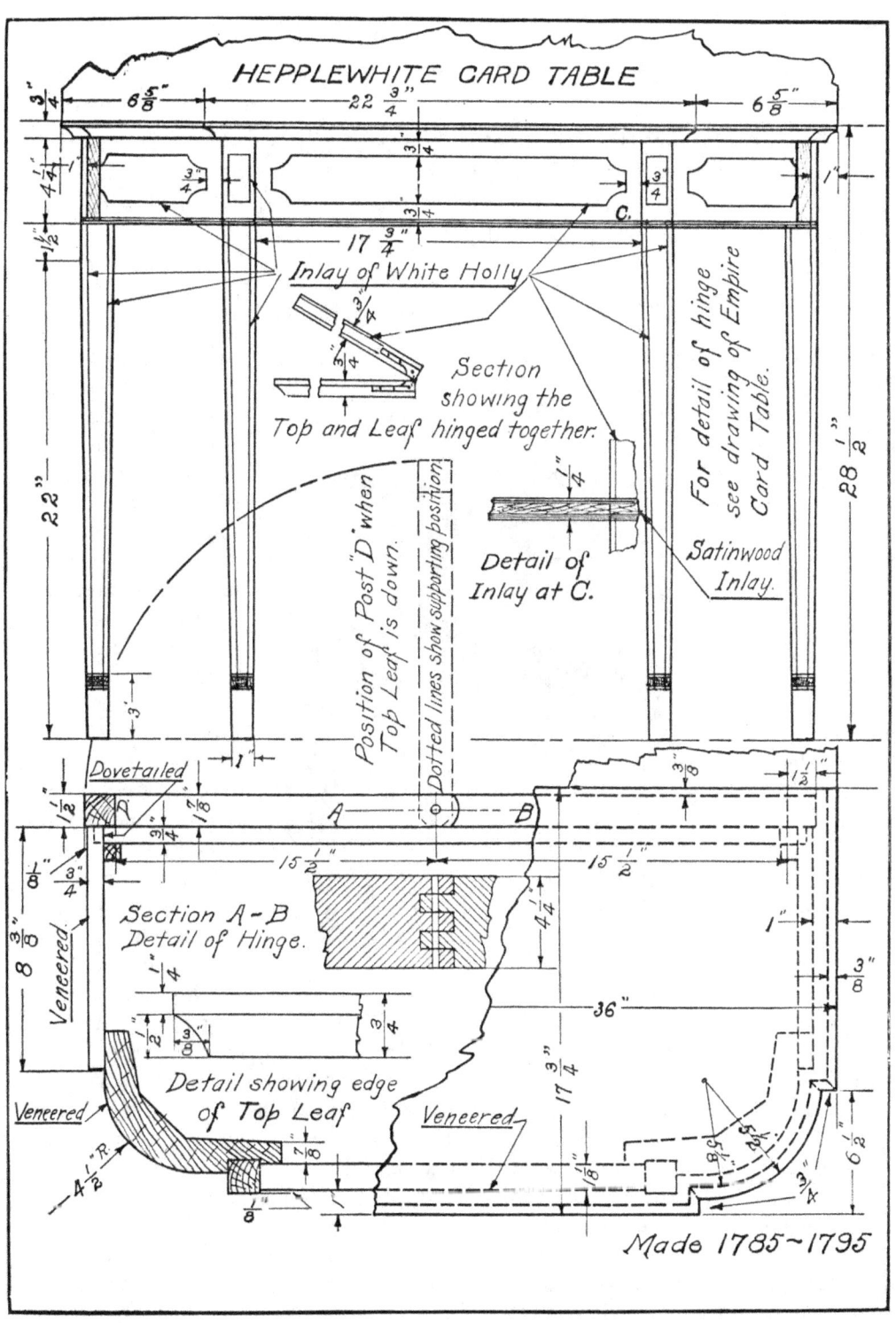

PLATE IX

EMPIRE CARD TABLE

THE Empire style followed the passing of the Hepplewhite and Sheraton designs. It is very easy to distinguish from the others. Sweeping curves, heavier construction and some carving can be found, which are the characteristics pertaining to this type. The early designs of the Empire are excellent, but the later ones were often made too heavy and after 1830 the style was gradually lost in the ugly shaped black walnut with which we are all so familiar.

DIRECTIONS FOR MAKING THE TABLE

The only departure from ordinary cabinet work in the making of this table is to prepare the four mahogany legs with the spiral or helical curves. After the posts are turned, the spirals can be marked on the post by laying out the pitch which is 6½ inches. A paper pattern of the curve can be used to develop the lines on the surface of the legs. To do this take a sheet of drawing paper which is about 7" wide and cut it 6½" long. Draw a line in the center of the paper perpendicular to the newly cut end. At one end of the paper measure the distance equal to the circumference of the leg where the spiral is to start, as at A—B, taking one half the distance in each direction from the center line. Now measure the circumference of the leg at C, and apply this measurement to the lower end of the paper in a similar manner. Connect points on the lower end with corresponding points on the upper end and cut on the lines. Now cut the paper on a diagonal, and either one of the pieces thus produced may be wrapped around the leg and a line drawn on the diagonal. This line will indicate the spiral to be cut. Shift this templet into a new position for each of the five spirals to be cut. Continue the lines to the lower end. Indent these lines with a sharp point and file to a depth of ⅛" and round over the edges to conform with the cross-section shown. Finish the process with sandpaper.

EMPIRE TABLE MADE ABOUT 1800. THE TOP IS PIVOTED AS SHOWN IN DRAWING

The posts are mortised to the rails which are pine. These are veneered with cross-grained mahogany. A compartment is built in on one side of the table and can only be reached by raising the table top. A wooden knob acts as a pivot, passing through a cross-piece which is mortised into the long rails. (See Fig. 8 page 29). Both table tops are ¾" thick and are rounded over along the edges. The hinges are of brass.

EMPIRE PERIOD CARD TABLE

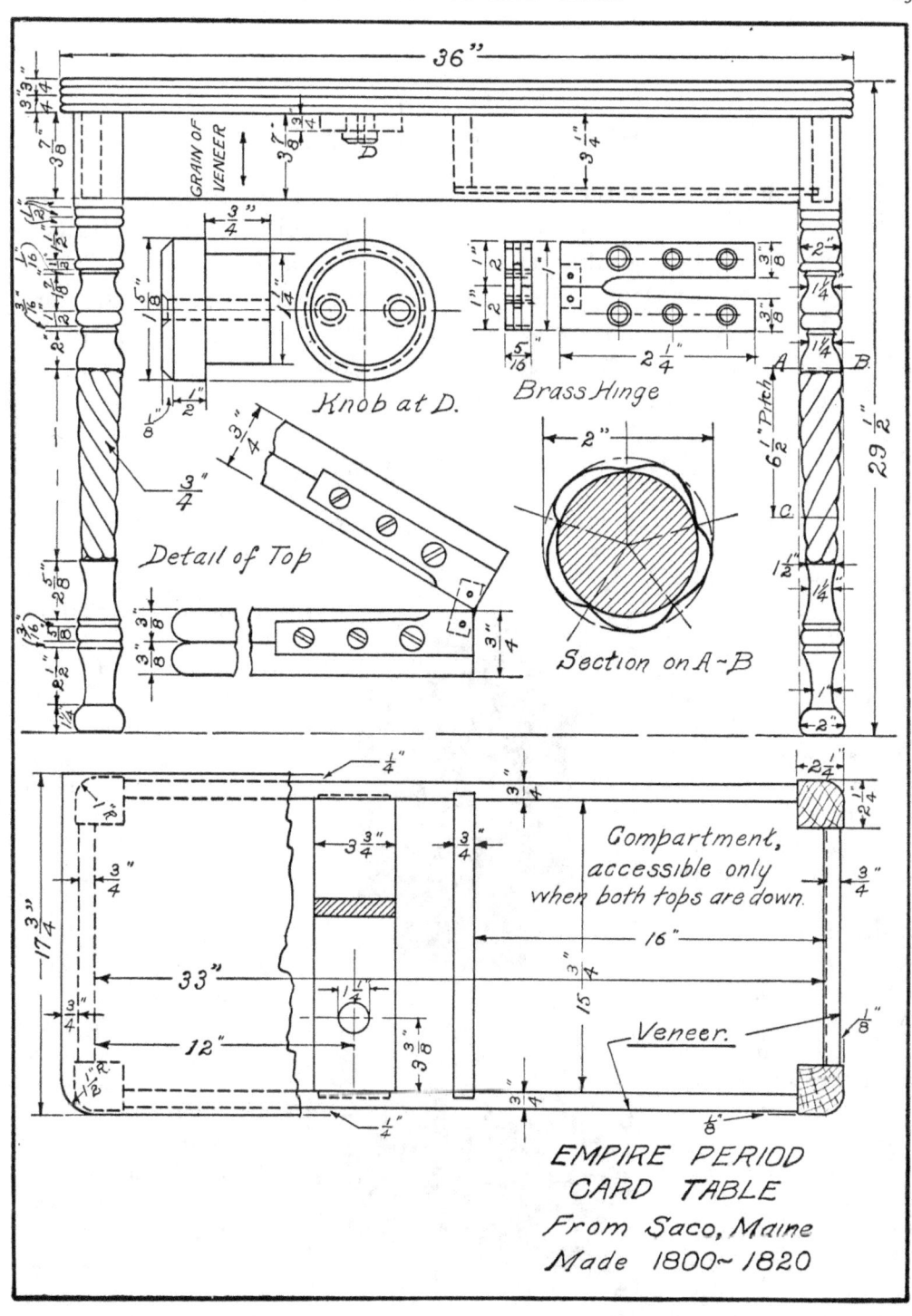

PLATE X

MAHOGANY TIP-TOP TABLE

THIS table is of a later period than the tea table shown on page 18. In reproducing this table in the Auburn high school, the drawing has been somewhat modified in order to obtain a more graceful curve in the design of the legs. The outer edges were rounded over in some cases and white holly lines were inlaid. These lines were $3/16''$ from the edge and $2''$ up from the bottom and $1''$ down from the upper end where the legs fit into the standard.

DIRECTIONS FOR MAKING THE TABLE

Lay out and cut the shape of the top on a piece of prettily grained mahogany. Prepare a piece of satinwood or curly grained maple to be used for the center of the marquetry. Set it in place on the top and scribe around it with a knife. Now carefully remove the wood between the lines and, with a router, level the place so that when the center is glued its top surface will be flush with the top of the table. When it is dry score knife lines around it and cut the groove for the border. Miter the corners.

Take the top over to the circular saw and cut away space for the $\frac{1}{2}''$ border. The cut should be equal to the thickness of the veneer and inlay. The next step is to glue the white holly line along the inner edge. Next place the cross-grained veneer in position. The corners must be mitered. Now even up the outer edge on the saw. After the work has been allowed to dry thoroughly, a narrow groove can be cut on the saw along the edge for the outside white holly lines. Use the same pattern in this groove as was placed around the marquetry.

The pedestal can now be turned on the lathe and the locating of the three feet is done the same way as for the mahogany tea table described on page 18. The shaping of the feet, making the maple block and the cleats are all mentioned in the same project and can be applied to this one.

Mahogany Tip-Top Table, Inlaid in Maple and Satin Wood

MAHOGANY TIP-TOP TABLE

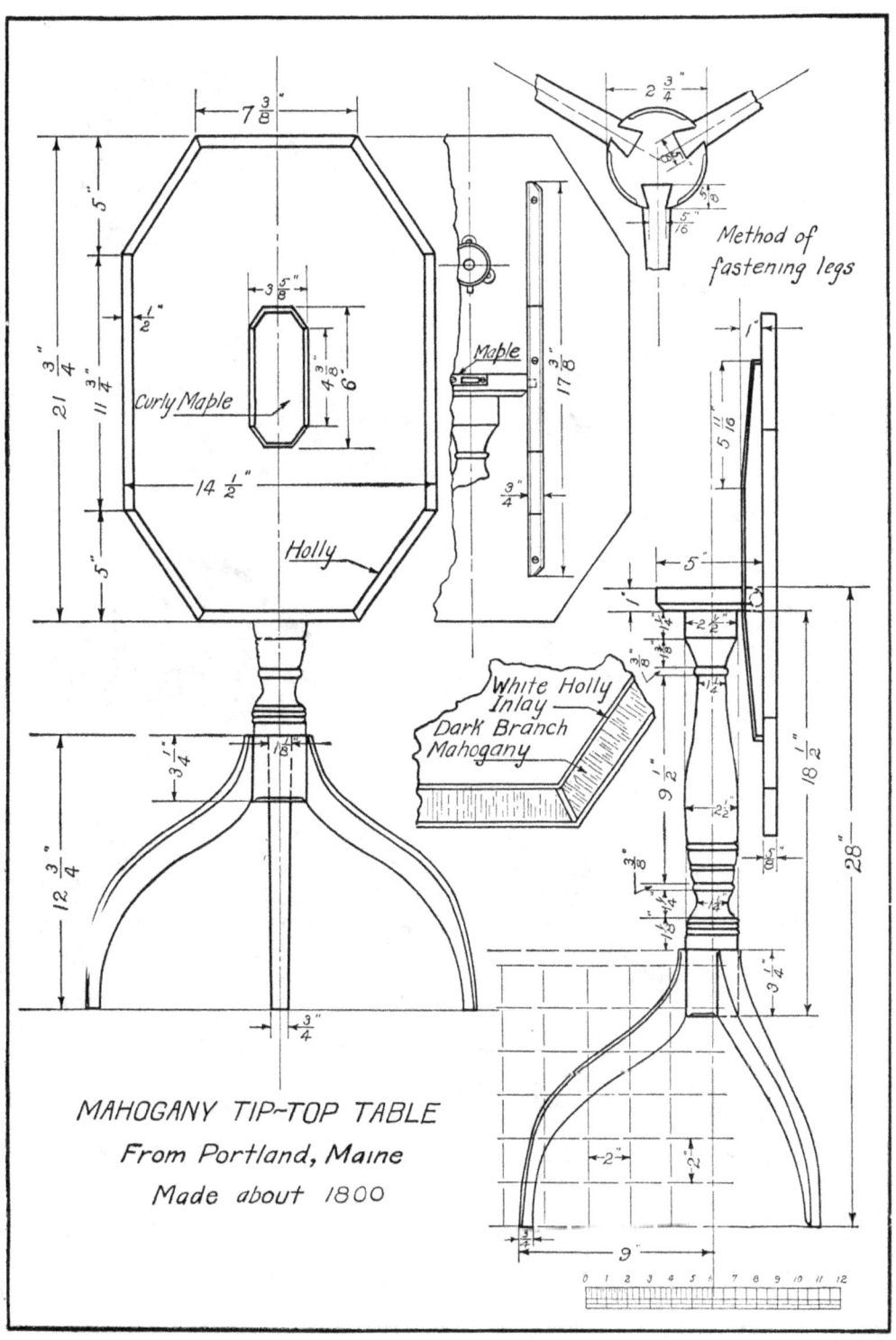

MAHOGANY TIP-TOP TABLE
From Portland, Maine
Made about 1800

PLATE XI

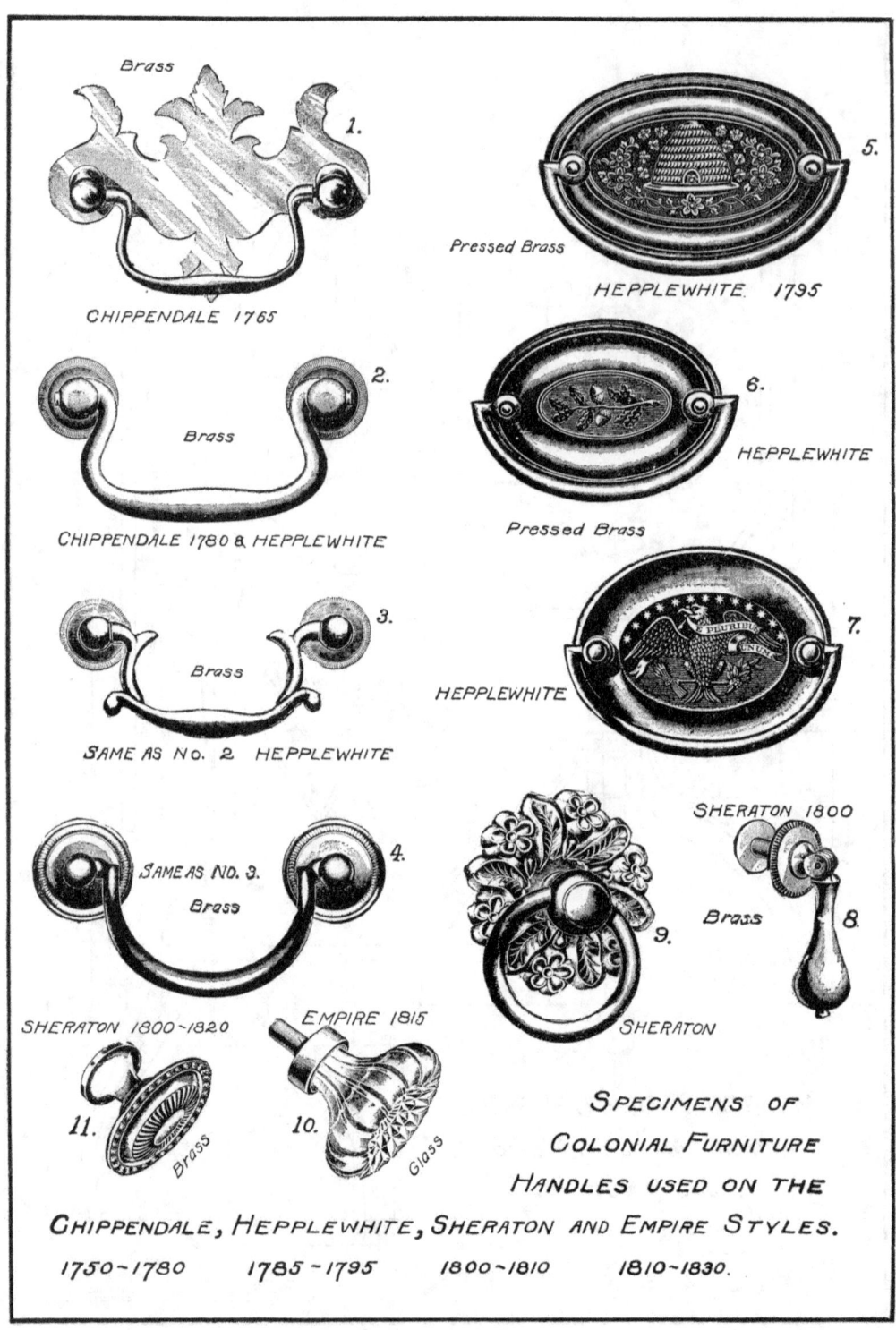

Plate XII

GENERAL DETAILS OF CONSTRUCTION

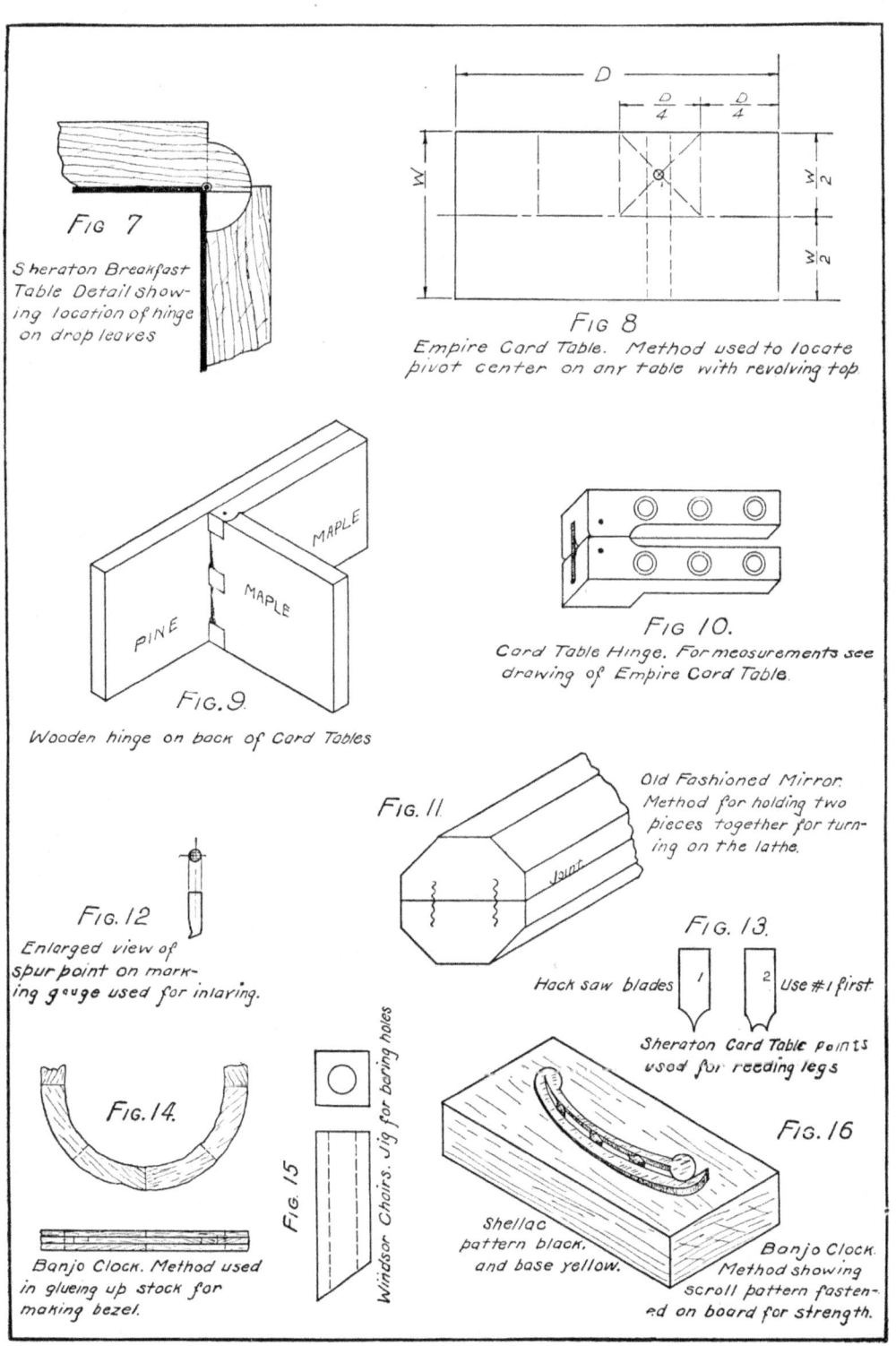

PLATE XIII

GRANDFATHER CLOCK

TALL clocks like old fashioned furniture can be traced by studying the design of the case and the works. The first ones were made with square shaped hoods or bonnets, dating as early as 1700. Later models were made with movements which have moving figures of ships, boats, or a miniature moon in her different phases. To make room for these extra parts, the arched top was added. Up to the time of the Revolutionary War most of the clock works were made of brass and imported from England. For some time afterward it was not possible to secure any more and so American clockmakers made their works of wood. Most of these clock makers were located in Connecticut. Terry, Hoadley, Harland, and Whiting were some of the manufacturers. It was the custom for clock peddlers to ride around the country and sell these wooden works. Quite often the movement was simply hung up on the wall and when more money was available, the local cabinet maker was called in to make a case. This is one of the reasons why hardly any two cases can be found alike. The best cases were made of

OLD FASHIONED GRANDFATHER CLOCK

mahogany with very elaborate carving and inlaying. The cheaper cases were generally made of pine and either painted or grained to imitate the better cabinet woods. Some very beautiful cases with brass movements were made by the leading clock makers and can be found running in perfect order today.

DIRECTIONS FOR MAKING THE CASE

This project is so large that it will be better to regard the making of the case as a separate undertaking. A complete case of mahogany will cost a little more but will be much more valuable. On the other hand, by using well seasoned stock a veneer of $\frac{1}{8}''$ can be placed on all outside surfaces. To start the case, shape up a board for the back 17'' wide and 6'-8¼'' long. Work out the outline and then build on the sides which have the heavy cleats 1⅝''x2¼'' along the upper edges. Put on the front which also has a cleat. Now place the long sides 7½″ wide and fasten them securely to the back of the case and to the cleats. On the inside, place corner blocks every 12″ apart. These sides stop 13¾″ from the top. The long narrow pieces on each side of the door are 2¾″ wide and extend 3″ above the upper moulding. Notch them before fastening to the case and mortise the cross rails above and below. Quarter-round mouldings fit into the notches and thin pieces of wood or brass should be located at the ends. Fluted or reeded corners will look better than the plain style which is shown on this case. Make up all the mouldings as shown in the sections. A cross rail is found just above the bonnet moulding on the case and is jointed to the 2¾″ stiles. Wooden supports are placed on the inside of the case to hold the works. The floor of the case is made of heavy stock owing to the strain that may be brought to bear upon it due to a falling weight.

DIRECTIONS FOR MAKING THE BONNET

The bonnet will prove to be a more difficult undertaking. As the sides are only 5/16″ thick it will be easier to make the arch first and join the sides to it. Commence where the round columns stop. Band-saw a piece of 1″ pine stock with an outside radius of 7″ and an inside radius of 5¼″. Dovetail both ends of this piece as shown on Plate XV. The front crown is of one piece 19½″ long and has a 7″ radius on the outside and 5⅜″ radius on the underside. It will take a piece of wood 2¼″ thick to make the arch. If the front surface for a thickness of ¾″ is mahogany, the rest of the material can be made of pine. This will permit shaping out the moulding without cutting thru into the pine. Sections C—D and Y, Plate XV, give the details. These can be worked out with a few gouges and sandpaper. The front and rear arches are connected with similar shaped mouldings 10″ long and mitered on the front end and dove-tailed at the rear. The top of the bonnet is covered with thin strips of wood which are reinforced with a piece of canvas or drilling. A mat of mahogany 5/16″ thick is set behind the door and is glued to the inside edge of the front arch (see Section C—D). The joints are half-lapped at the top and bottom and the width of the mat is 14¼ inches. Now get out the base moulding of the bonnet (section R, Plate XVI) and the sides. Connect the base, sides and arch, and put in the back corner pieces and quarter-round corners. The round columns belong on the front. Brass caps and bases hold them in place. The door is made of mahogany ¾″ thick with mitered corners. The door hinges are nothing more than two small pieces of brass, shaped and located as shown on Plate XVI. Two small brass round-head screws are put into the underside of the arch and down on the base moulding, passing thru the brass hinges on the right hand side. The windows on the sides are 3″ by 5″ and are held in place with cleats on the inside.

There are three ornamental posts on the top. The broken arch is jointed in back of the center post and the grain should run diagonally. This clock case has three ornamental mahogany urns which are placed on top of the posts. Usually they are made of brass. The inlay around the front of the case is detailed on Plate XVI and directions for setting it in place may be found on the pages pertaining to the card tables, particularly on page 23.

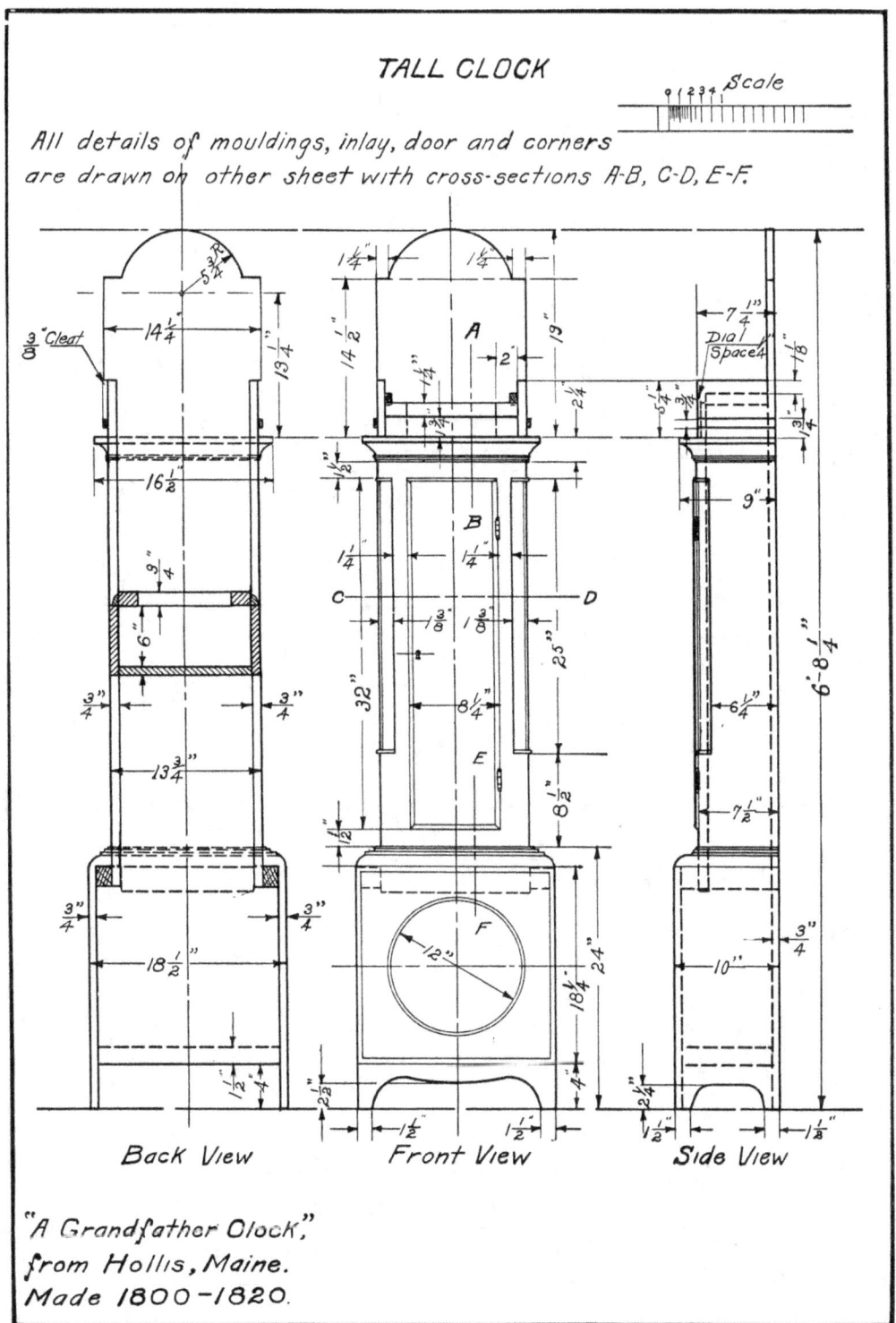

Plate XIV

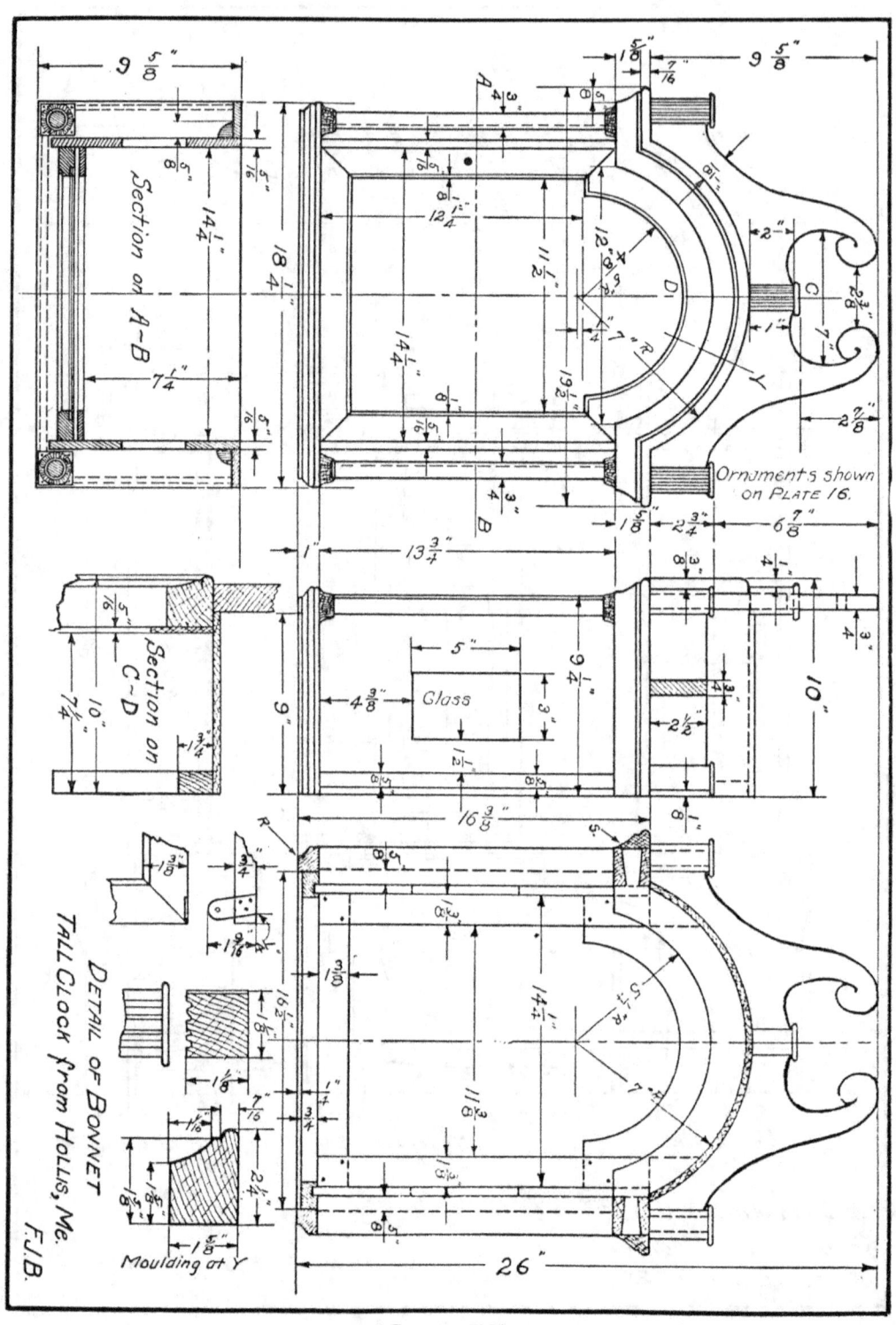

Plate XV

GRANDFATHER CLOCK

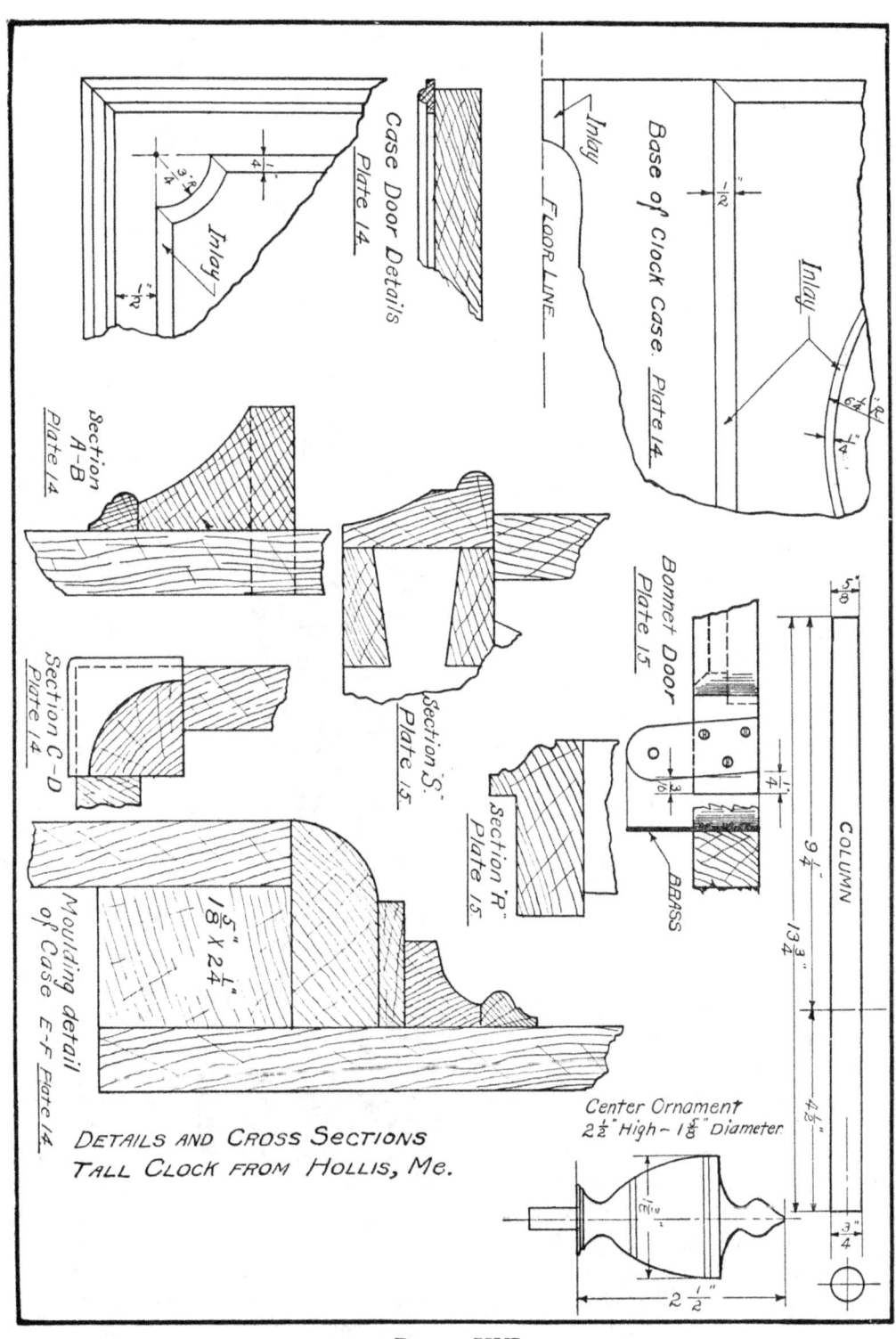

PLATE XVI

BANJO CLOCK

THE banjo clocks are among the new styles which are attracting attention at present. This design of a small clock case was first made and sold by the famous Willards of Boston. There were at least four clock makers by this name and the most highly prized of all banjo clocks are the ones made by them. The first ones were made about 1802. Reproductions are made in quantities now and in all sizes, from the small 2" dials to the size of the one given on this drawing.

DIRECTIONS FOR MAKING THE CASE

Perhaps the wisest thing to do would be to purchase the movement first. Then if any dimensions on this drawing are not suited, slight alterations can be made without affecting the design. The back should be worked out first. It is $\frac{3}{8}$" thick and about 30" long. Put a center line down thru the middle of it and locate each part, the head and box. Draw the outline of the back which extends $\frac{3}{16}$" beyond the case on all sides and band-saw to shape. Construct a box with mitered and splined corners and glue in place on the backboard. The head is made of two thick pieces of mahogany and is turned on the outside. The opening for the works can be band-sawed as space for the pendulum walls must be cut out. These walls pass from under the dial bezel, down thru the box to the bottom. The bezel should be made up with three courses of segments to prevent it from warping (see Fig. 14, page 29). A hinge on the right hand side and a catch on the left hand hold it in place. The pendulum bezel can be made of single thickness stock with mitered corners. The upper ends are left longer than the space to be covered so that the dial bezel will hold it. The box bezel is mitered and has two hinges and a clasp. The top ornament is made of wood and is square. A small brass eagle with outstretched wings is often found on clocks of this kind. The overhanging edge of the back should be rounded over.

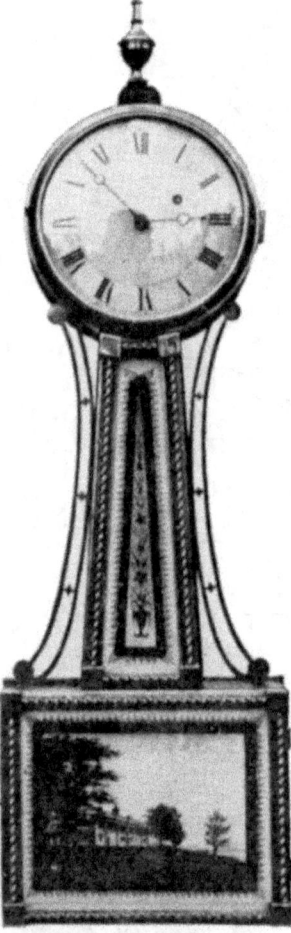

A BANJO CLOCK OF THIS DESIGN MAY BE MADE TO SUIT ANY SIZE MOVEMENT

Two brass scrolls are placed on each side of the case, so it will be necessary to make a wood pattern in order to secure the castings. The best way is to make a full size lay-out of the scroll on a piece of pine (see Fig. 16, page 29) about 6" wide. Cut the outline of the scroll on pine, $\frac{5}{32}$" thick and glue it on the board. Have the edges smooth and allow enough draft so that the pattern will draw clean from the mold. It would be a difficult task for any molder to handle such a delicate pattern unless it were fastened to a

BANJO CLOCK

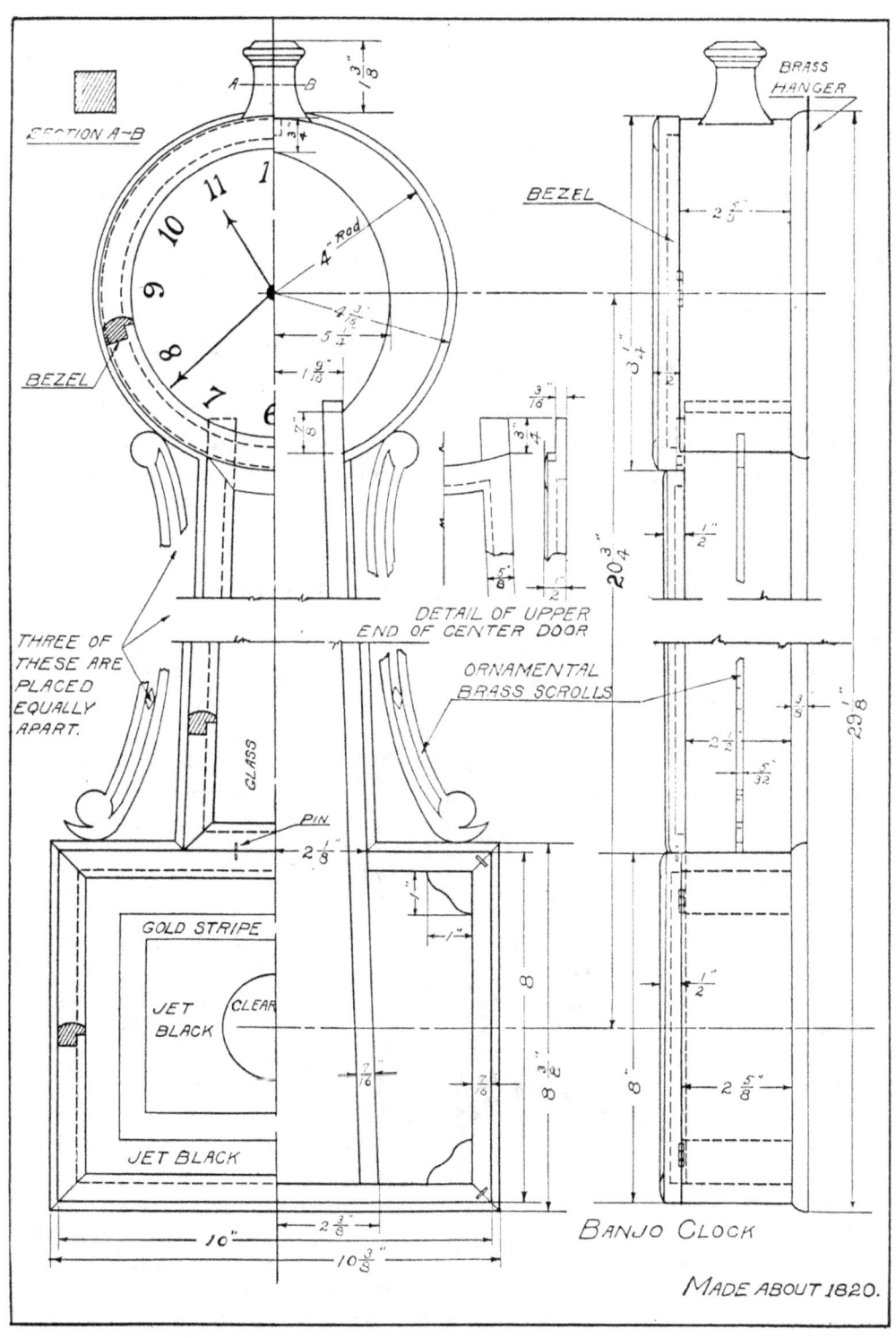

Plate XVII

board. File the castings smooth and lacquer with very thin yellow shellac. If it is not convenient to make the patterns and castings, wooden scrolls can be used. They are not so attractive but were not uncommon on banjo clocks.

WINDSOR CHAIRS

WINDSOR chairs were first made in England. They were very common during the Colonial days. The seats were made of pine and the backs of some kind of hardwood as ash or hickory. Quite a few furniture dealers can now furnish reproductions of the Windsor styles in mahogany with more comfortable lines and nicer finish than the older types, which makes them very desirable. The directions given below are suited for any of the Windsor chairs which are included in this series.

DIRECTIONS FOR MAKING THE CHAIR

Make the seat first, locating the centers for the holes where the legs are to set in place on the underside. Use wooden jigs as illustrated in Fig. 15, page 29, for boring the holes at the proper angles. Bevel the edges of the seat and hollow the top surface so that it looks and feels comfortable. Do not bore the holes through the seat unless the drawings show them that way. Turn the legs and rounds on the lathe and attach them to the seat. The rim for the fan-shaped backs can be bent on a form marked out on a work-table or on the floor. Make a full size lay-out of the shape of the back and nail small blocks every 6" apart to hold the rim in place. Steam or soak the rim in hot water and place it in the form where it should be left for at least 36 hours. When it is thoroughly dry, remove it and fit it to the holes on the seat. Pass the ends through to the under side of the seat and split the ends open and drive in wooden wedges. Shape up the spindles with a spokeshave and bend on a form. When they are ready, bore the holes through the rim and push the spindles up through the holes. Then place glue in the holes on the seat and pull the spindles down into place. When the glue is dry, cut the projecting ends off

WINDSOR CHAIR

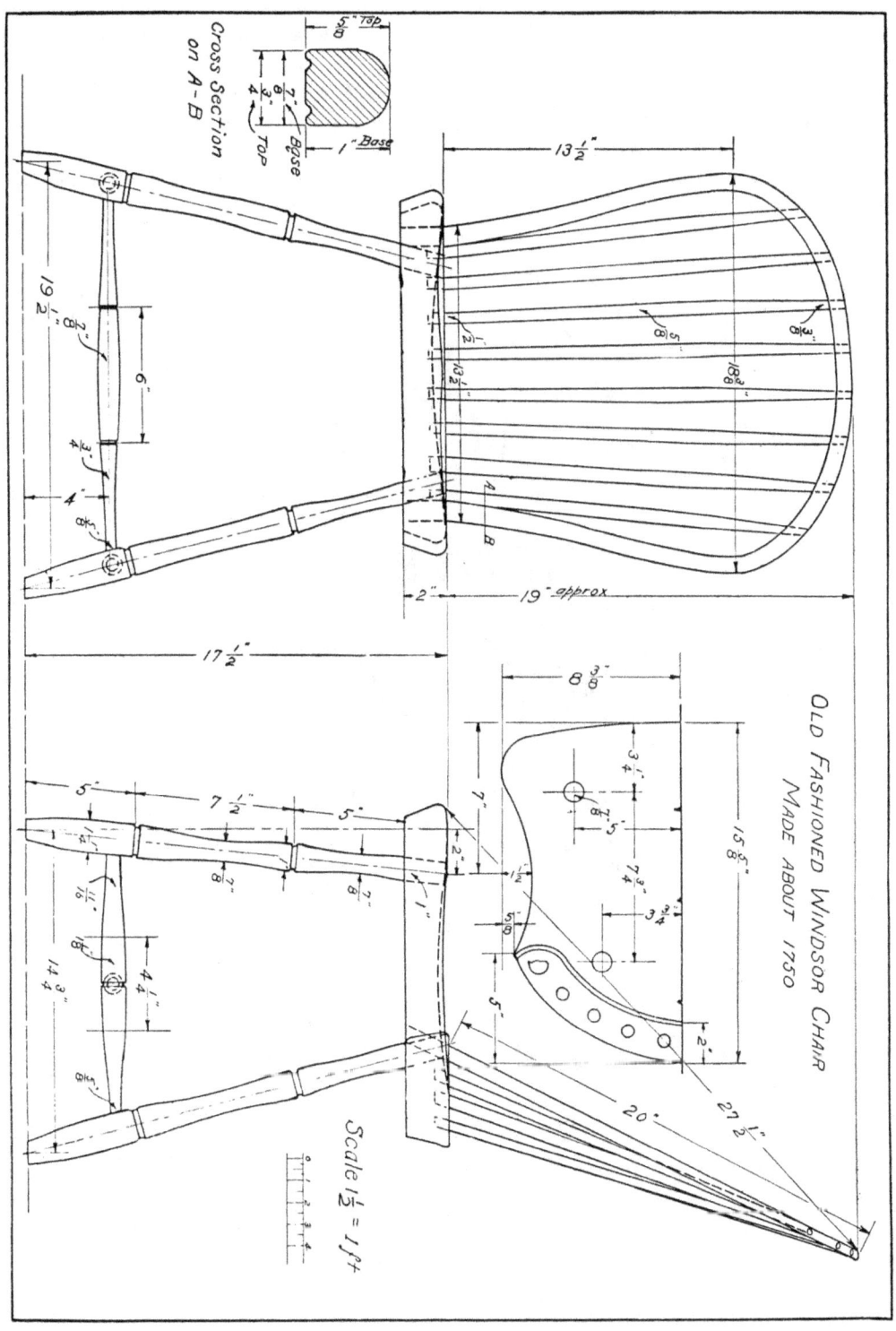

Plate XVIII

so that they are even with the outside of the rim. Sandpaper all parts and paint the chair with two coats of black enamel. The small ridges or grooves on the legs and spindles should be colored with two or more coats of gilt or bronze paint. These finishing directions refer to the chair if pine and ash are used in its construction.

The drawings on pages 39 to 42 show Winsor chairs of varied details. The method of construction is largely the same as described above. If mahogany is used, see page 52.

Windsor Chairs were Used in Colonial Days. They are Again Becoming Popular and can now be had in Various Details and Finishes

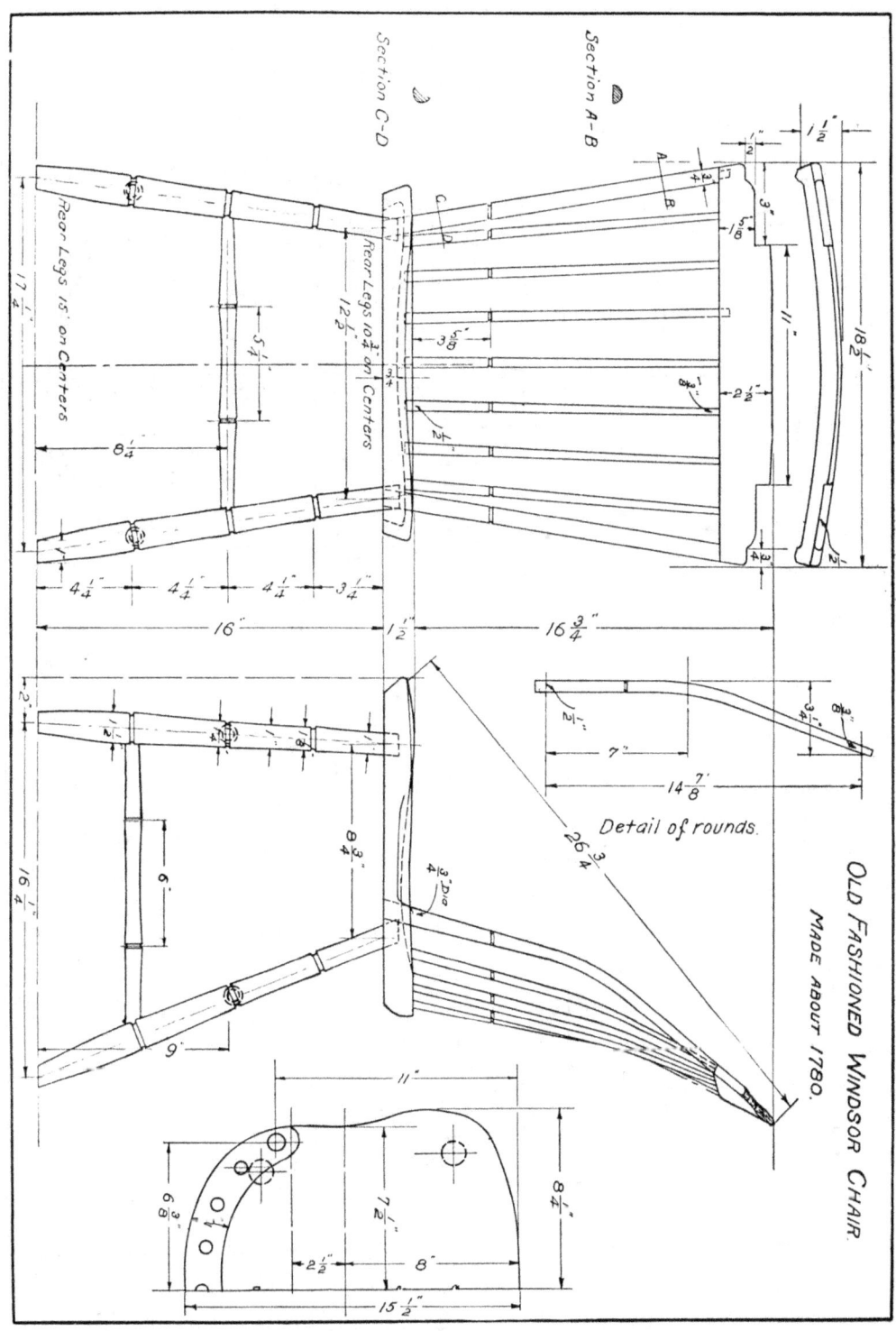

PLATE XIX

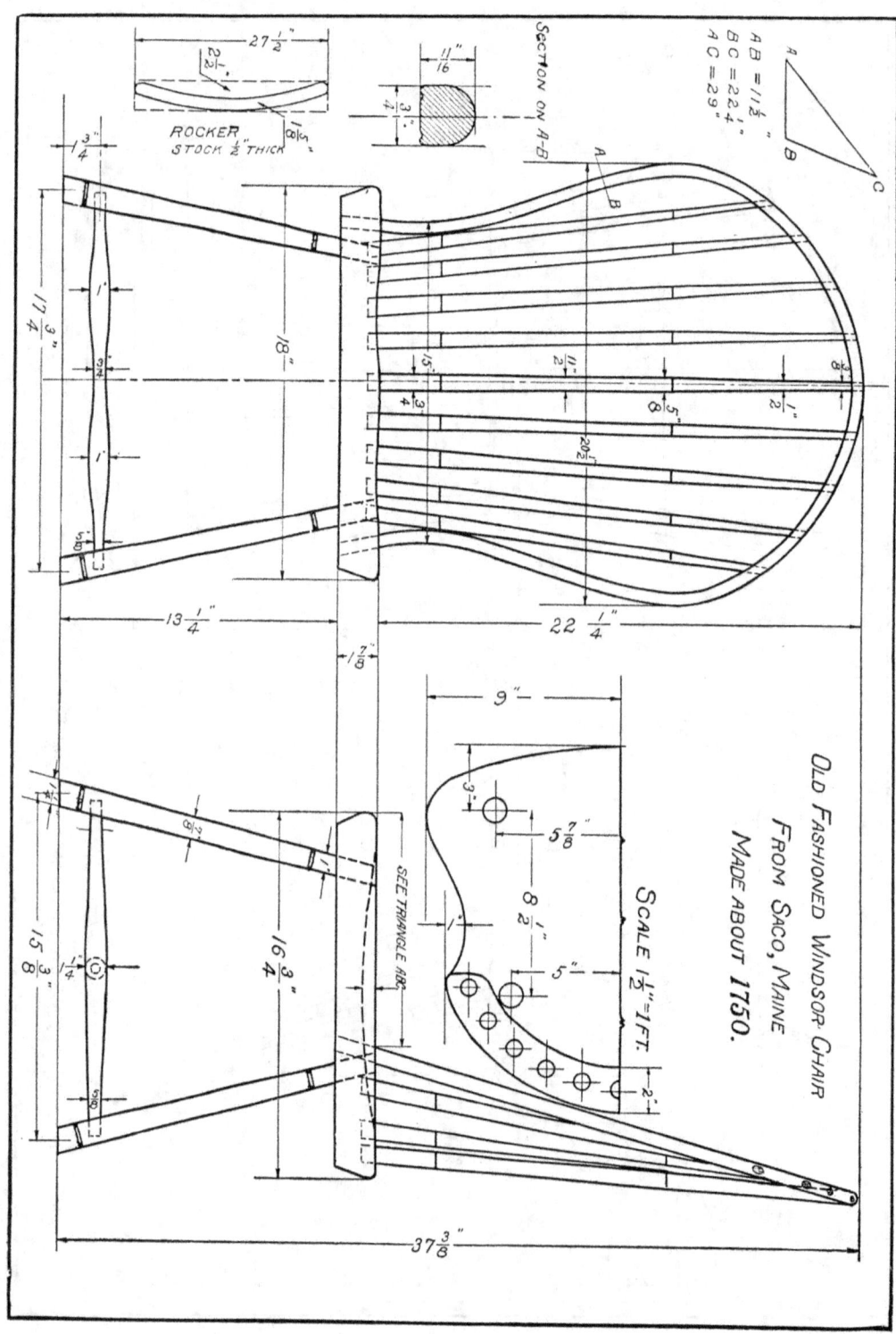

Plate XX

CHAIR DETAILS

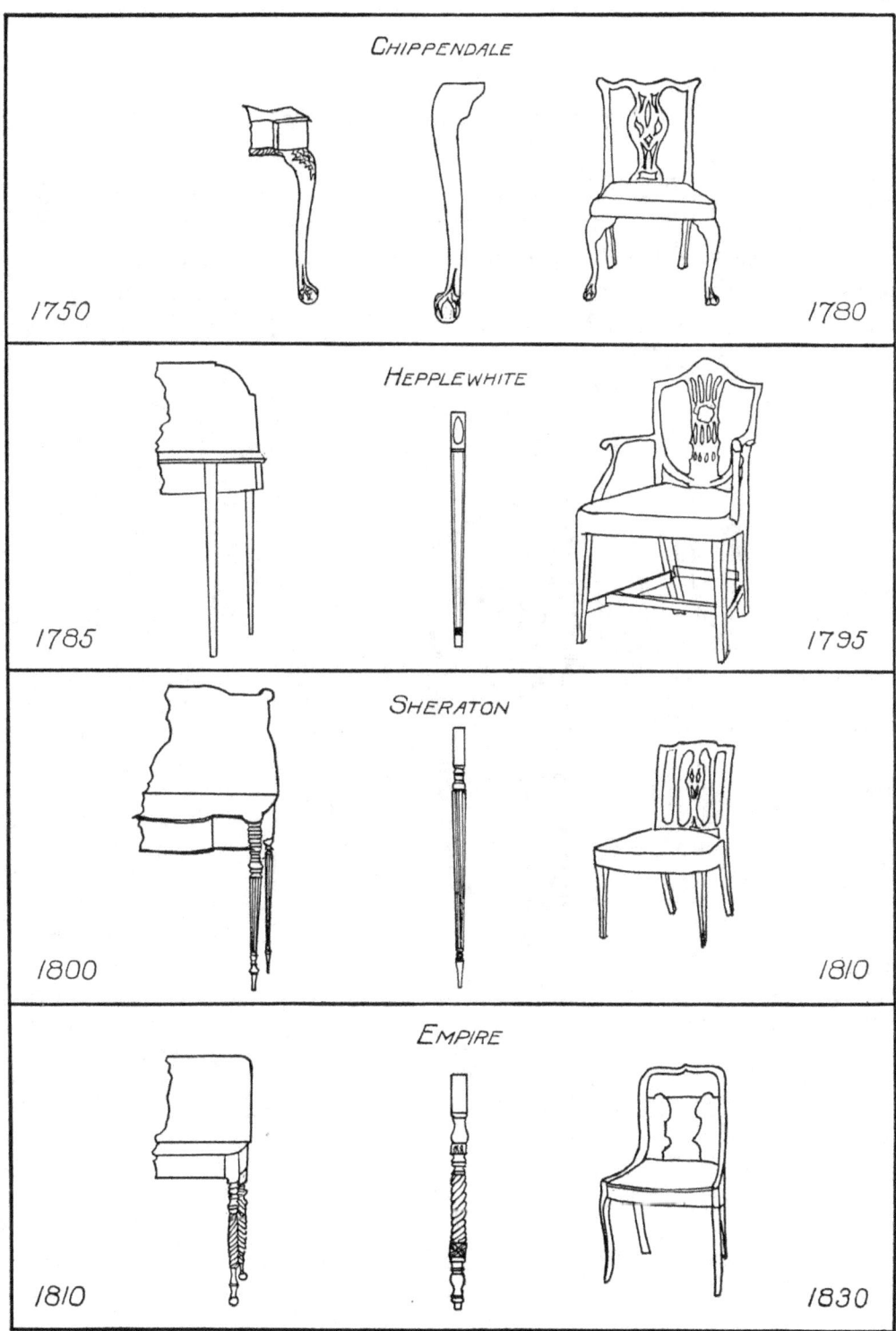

Plate XXI

HEPPLEWHITE CHAIR

SOME of the finest chairs in existence were made from the designs of Hepplewhite. They are noted for their fine delicately shaped outlines with beautiful inlaying and shield-shaped backs. Mahogany is used and the seats are upholstered. The chairs are rather fragile and cannot compare with the Chippendale and Windsor styles for strength and durability.

DIRECTIONS FOR MAKING THE CHAIR

THE HEPPLEWHITE CHAIR IS MARKED BY THE SHIELD-SHAPED BACK AND FINE INLAY

The joints of the chair from the seat down are all mortised and tenoned. The back can be reproduced by drawing 2" squares on a sheet of heavy paper and checking off the intersections on the drawing. After drawing the outline, cut it out and use it for a pattern. The back legs are extended above the seat, making a total length of not less than 36". First one side is band-sawed and then the other. Use the waste pieces to form a cradle when making the second cut. The back shield is jointed at the bottom and a piece of wood ¾" thick is fitted into the corner. The slats are housed into this piece and also to the under side of the rim above. Corner blocks are placed under the cushion to reinforce the frame of the chair. A white holly line is inlaid around the middle of the rim and is represented by a heavy black line on the drawing. Cross-sections at *A—B* and *C—D* will show the shape of the rim.

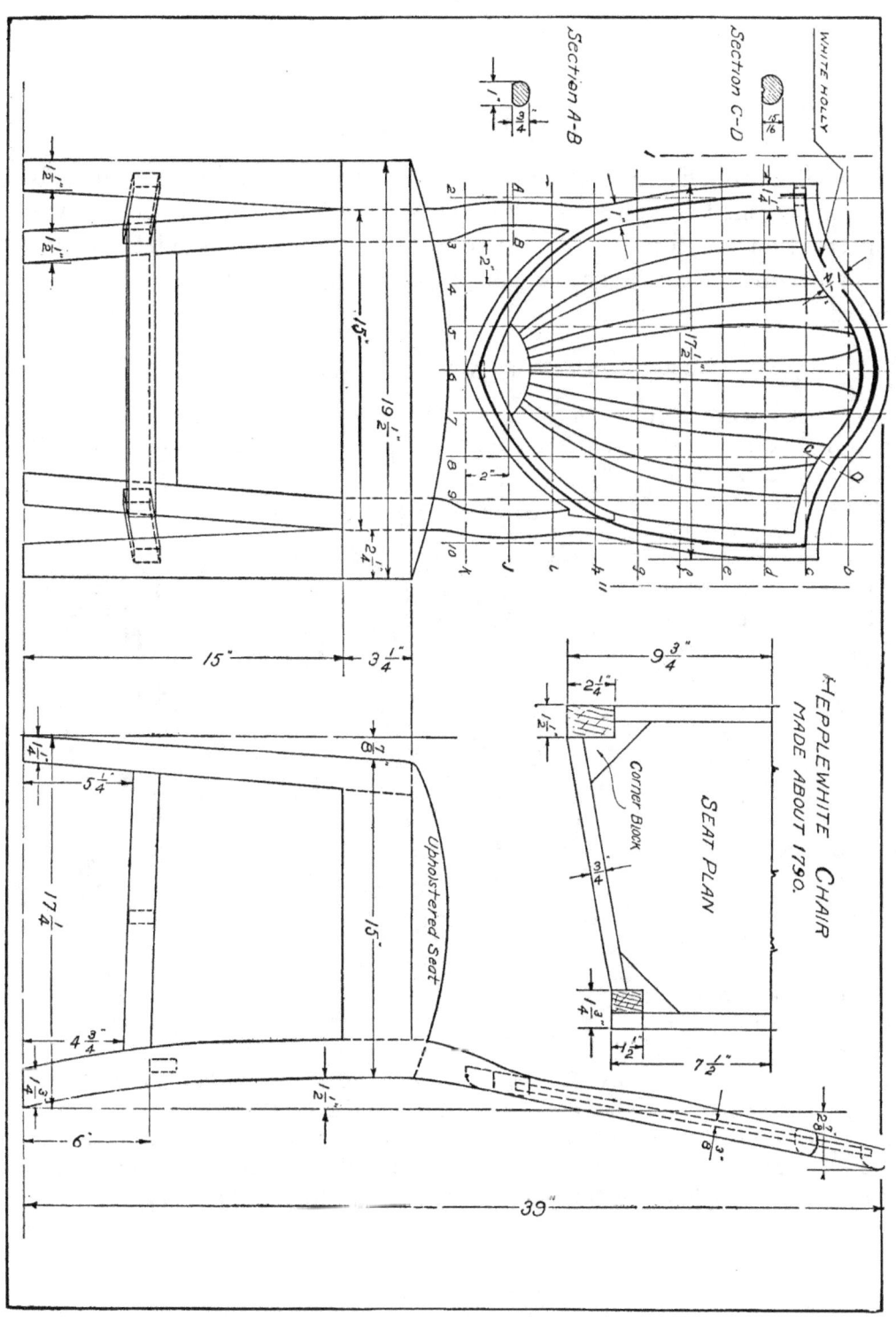

Plate XXII

EMPIRE CHAIR

THE Early Empire chairs are very pretty and are easily distinguished from the other periods. Sweeping curves and heavier construction are some of the notable features. Later models are less valuable due to unattractive carvings and jig saw work which were added.

DIRECTIONS FOR MAKING THE CHAIR

The back legs of this chair can be made of single thickness mahogany, from the floor line up to the point marked *J* on the drawing. All joints from here down are mortised and tenoned. The front and back rails are made of oak and band-sawed to shape. They are then veneered with cross-grained mahogany. Section *C—D* shows a quarter-round piece of mahogany along the top edge of the front rail and a thin piece attached to the underside. A mortise ¼" wide and ¼" deep, is cut into the back rail to receive the middle panel which connects with the seat frame and the curved back. The back is mortised to the back legs at *J* and has a veneered surface and a raised edge which can be glued on and rounded over to the shape shown in the section. The middle panel is cut from a piece of burl-grained wood and may have to be

Windsor Chair   Empire Chair

steamed or soaked in hot water to fit it into the grooves. The cushion is removable and is covered with chintz. The frame of the cushion is made of oak and rests on the front and back rails.

EMPIRE CHAIR

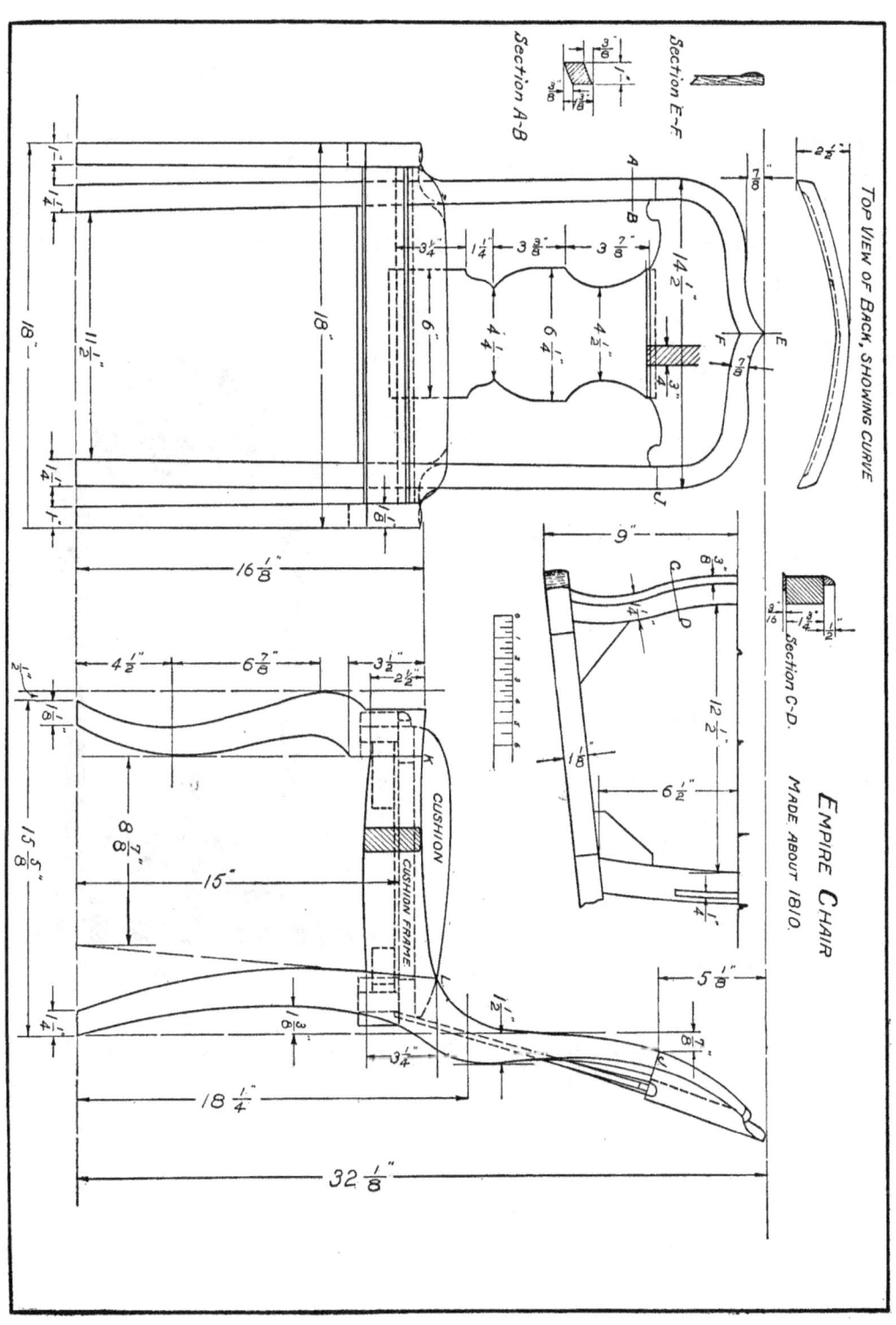

Plate XXIII

COLONIAL LOOKING GLASS

THIS is one of the styles which can be associated with the Chippendale and Hepplewhite periods. The frames are made of mahogany and are often embellished with gilt work around the scrolls. The sizes vary a great deal. Most of them are about one-third as large as this one.

DIRECTIONS FOR MAKING THE FRAME

Make a mahogany frame of stock which is ¾″ thick and 1¼″ wide. Cut some cross-grained wood on the circular saw ⅛″ thick, 6″ wide and 1″ long, and glue it to the face of the frame, mitering the corners. Take a piece of cardboard and mark it off in $2\frac{7}{16}''$ squares. Copy the scroll for the top, sides and base of the frame and cut the outline. Use burl-grained wood ⅜″ thick and dowel and glue it to the frame. The grain of the side pieces should run in the same direction as the top piece. When the glue is dry, place the card-board patterns on the wood and mark the outline. Take the frame to the band-saw and cut close to the lines. Smooth up the edges, round over the arrises of the frame and the project is ready for staining and finishing.

COLONIAL LOOKING GLASS

A very neat little frame can be made from the same design by planning to use a mirror measuring 7″ x 11″.

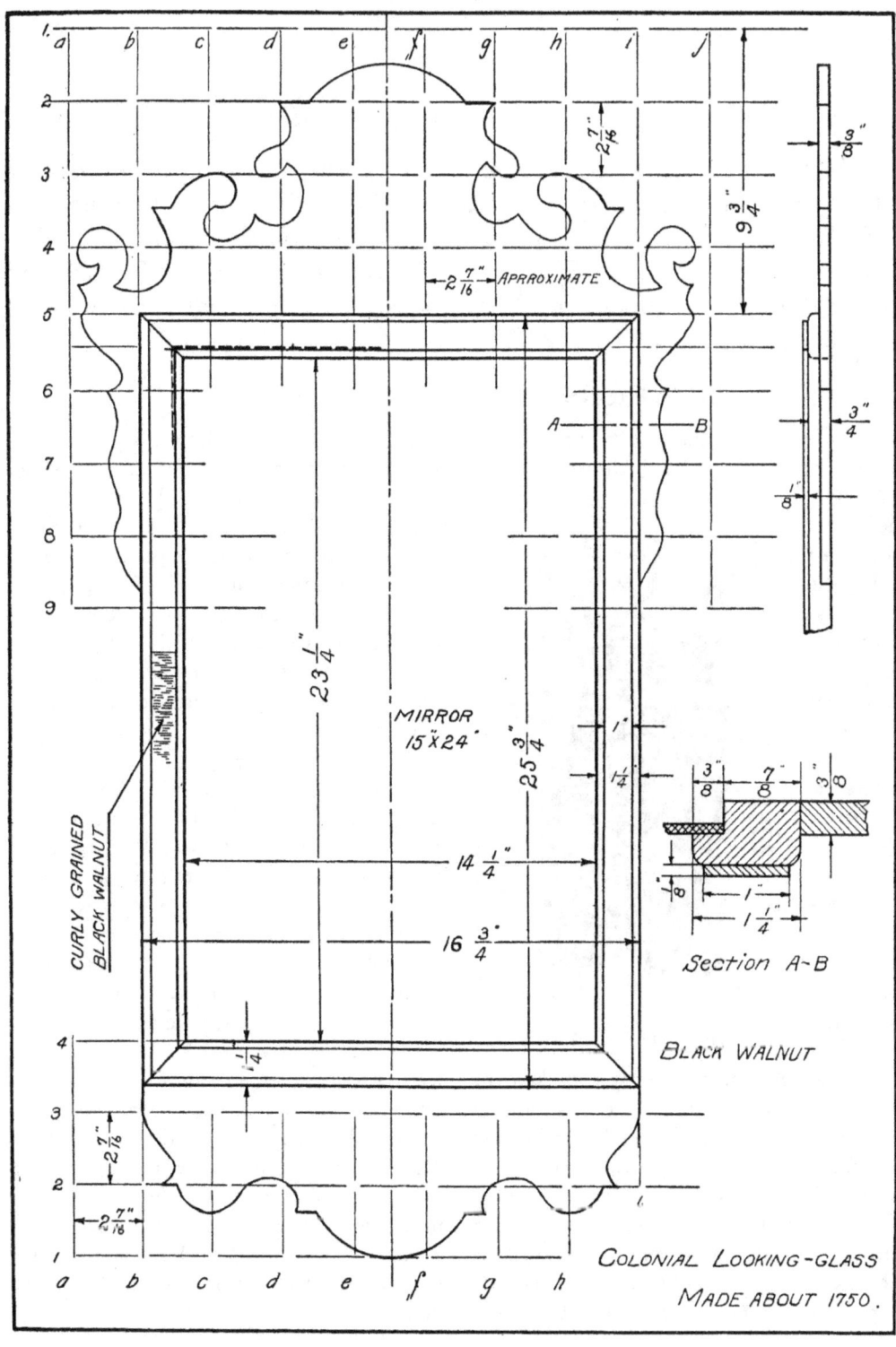

Plate XXIV

OLD FASHIONED MIRROR

THIS is a style which developed during the Empire period and is a great favorite today. Students beginning wood-turning will find this project a good application of some of the exercise models which are usually made. The finish is quite an important feature and calls for gold leaf, but for a school project a fairly good substitute is a bronze or gilt paint.

DIRECTIONS FOR MAKING THE FRAME

This frame is made like any other picture frame, with or without mitered corners as the blocks will cover and lock the joints. The partition strip across the frame must be rabbeted on both edges to include the picture and the mirror. The original frame has small stamped brass rosettes tacked to the corner blocks, but if they cannot be made or obtained, each block can be put on a face-plate in the lathe and turned.

The half-round spindles on the sides and ends of the frame are made in the lathe. For the long pieces, take two pieces of pine ¾"x 1½" and at least 24" long. Glue or fasten them together (see Fig. 11, page 29) at the ends and at one spot near the middle. Locate the exact centers of the joints on both ends and place the piece in the lathe. Turn down the wood to the right shape as though it were a solid piece of wood. Sandpaper as smooth as possible and then remove the wood from the lathe. With a thin bladed knife, pry the two pieces apart and then fit each piece to the sides of the frame. The spindles for the top and bottom are made in the same way.

Parts of the frame are finished in gold and the rest in black. These places are so noted on the drawing. Put about a teaspoon of lampblack into a cup of orange or yellow shellac. Stir thoroly and apply a little on a clean piece of pine. If the color is not a jet black, add more lampblack. It will take at least two coats to make the frame look right. The corner blocks are gilded on the top surface if there are no rosettes, and black along the edges. The rest of the frame is gilded.

The old mirrors generally had colored pictures placed in the upper space and were painted directly on the glass. Colonial scenes were the most common. A colored picture of Mt. Vernon will look very well in this frame and can be placed behind clear glass.

Old Fashioned Mirror

OLD FASHIONED MIRROR

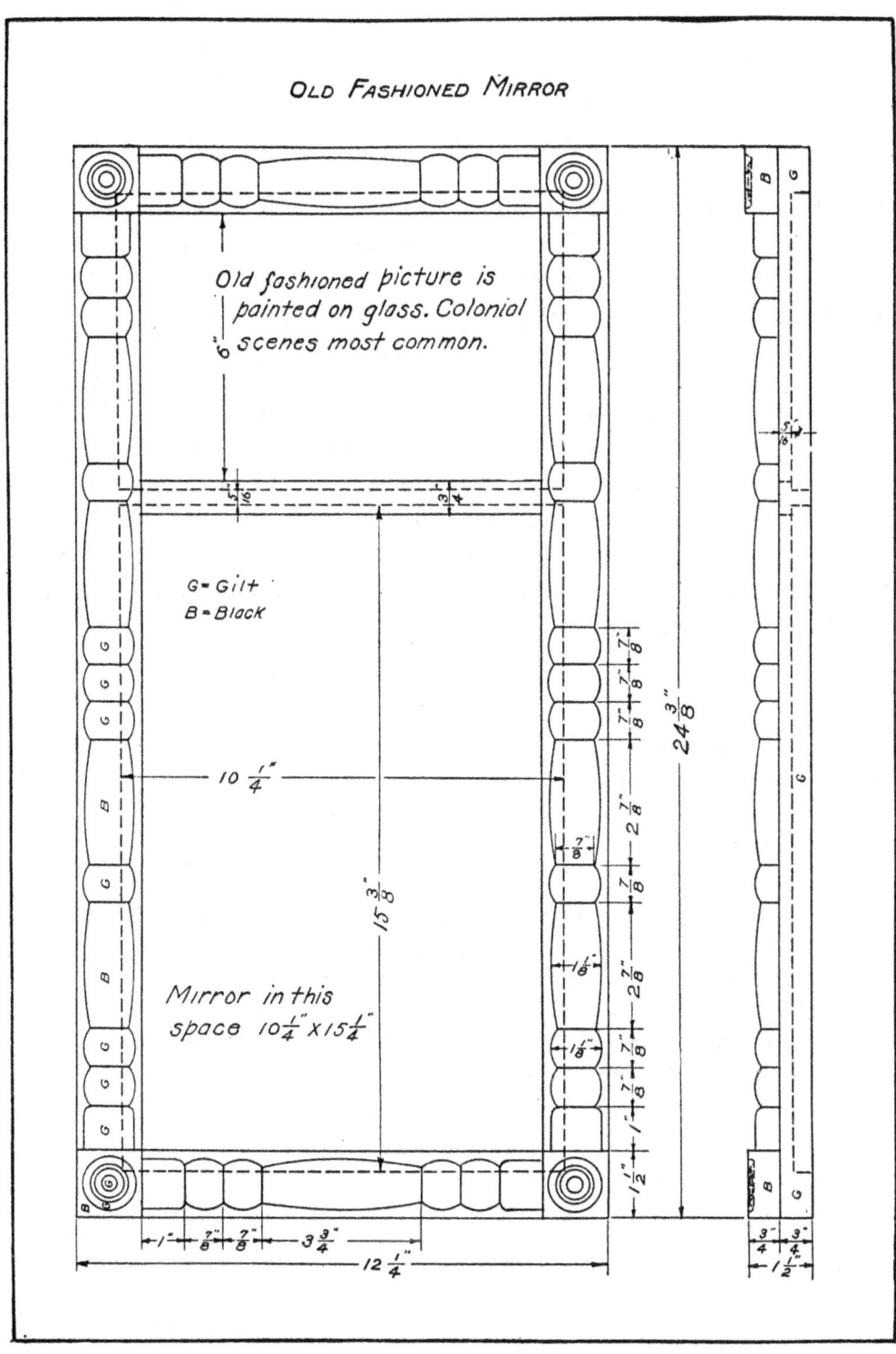

Plate XXV

WOOD FINISHING

THE author considers it expedient to say a few words about the finishing of the reproductions which may be made from the drawings, more especially because much of the mahogany sold is commercially known as baywood. The mahogany antique pieces which were measured are made of San Domingo mahogany and because of its deep reddish natural color does not require any staining. Baywood on the other hand, is likely to be a pale brown color, and while not as desirable, it can be stained and finished to look very well. The outlined methods may not be in accordance with the best practices of the finishing room, but will serve for school shop purposes. They are based on observations made in antique shops where old fashioned pieces were being restored and thru experiments and results of making reproductions from these drawings by students.

FINISHING

1. Sandpaper all parts smooth.
2. Apply one coat potassium bichromate solution.
3. Apply second coat if needed.
4. Sandpaper very lightly.
5. Shellac inlay lines and borders. Use white shellac.
6. Apply one coat of dark mahogany oil stain.
7. Apply six or more coats of very thin orange shellac. Rub each coat down with pumic stone and oil. Rub last coat with rotten stone and oil. Use no varnish on any of these projects.

Potassium bichromate solution: Dissolve ¼ oz. of potassium bichromate in one pint of hot water. Use cold, and test on piece of scrap wood. When dry, the color of the wood will show a dull cocoa brown. A weak solution will not discolor the inlay. The latter should be carefully shellacked, however, before the stain is applied.

INDEX

A
Arch, broken 32

B
Bands, ebony 14, 20
Base, tripod 18
Bevel, concave 22
Bezel, clock 36, 37
Bonnet, for tall clock 31, 32, 34
Brackets, wooden 14
Brass 22, 28, 32

C
Catch, spring 19
Cauls, wooden 12
Chairs 38, 44, 46
    Bannister back 6
    Empire 46, 47
    Hepplewhite 44, 45
    Windsor 38, 39, 40, 41, 42
Chippendale, designs 28, 43
Clockmakers 31, 36
Clocks, Tall or Grandfather 31, 36
    Banjo 36, 37
Colonial Days 18, 38, 40
Colonial Looking Glass 48, 49
Columns, round 32
Compartments 20, 21, 24

D
Details 29
Dividers, use of 18
Dovetails 18, 20, 22
Drawers 7, 12, 20, 21
Drawer pulls 28

E
Ebony 14, 15, 19, 21
Edges, beaded 7
English clocks 31

F
Feet, for tables 20, 26
File, used in inlaying 14
Finishing, wood 7, 16, 40, 50, 52

G
Gates 7
Gouges 32
Grain, of wood 18, 21
Gumwood 7

H
Handles, specimens of 28
Hinges, metal 7, 12, 14, 22, 23, 25, 26, 36
    wooden 14, 15, 22, 29
Hepplewhite 10, 14, 20, 22, 28, 43, 44
Holly, white 14, 15, 19, 26

I
Inlay 11, 14, 15, 18, 20, 21, 22, 23

J
Jigs, wooden 38

K
Knob, wooden 12
Knurls 11

L
Lampblack 50
Lay-out
    for tavern table 16
    for banjo clock 36
    for Windsor chair 38
Leaves, table 7

M
Mahogany 7, 10, 12, 14, 18, 20, 24, 26, 32, 46, 48
Maple 7, 11, 13, 15, 22, 26, 27, 31
Marking gage
    used in inlaying 14, 22
    used in scoring 18
Marquetry 26
Mirrors, old fashioned 48, 49, 50, 51
Mouldings 32
Mt. Vernon, picture of 50

O
Oak 7
Ornaments,
    for banjo clock 36
    for clock bonnet 35

P
Panels 12
Pattern, wood, for brass scrolls 36
Pedestal, for tables 18, 20, 26
Penn, William 7
Pins, wooden 17, 18
Pine 7, 12, 14, 22
Poplar 7
Pulls, drawer 7, 12, 28

R
Reproductions, of furniture 7, 10, 12, 16
Router 26

S
Satinwood 12, 23, 26
Segments 36
Shellac, black 14
    orange 50
    white 38, 50, 52
Sheraton 10, 28, 43
Snake-foot, for table construction 18
Spindles 50

INDEX

	Page
Spur, of marking gage	14, 22
Standard, for table	26
Steel, points for reeding	10
Steel-square	7
Stock, five-ply	20
Straight-edge, used in reeding	10
Styles, Period	43

T

	Page
Tables, Empire Card	11, 24, 25
Gate-leg	6, 7, 8, 9
Hepplewhite Card	22, 23
Hepplewhite Work	20, 21
Mahogany Tea	18, 19
Mahogany Tip-top	26, 27
Sheraton Breakfast	14, 15
Sheraton Card	10, 11
Sheraton Work	12, 13
Tavern	7, 16, 17
Tapers	14, 15, 22, 25

V

	Page
Veneers	12, 14, 22, 25

W

	Page
Walnut	7, 49
War, Revolutionary	31
Wood finishing	52
Wood-turning	50
Works, wooden clock	31